SO-AXJ-232

# WINNING THE TECHNOLOGY TALENT WAR

# WINNING THE TECHNOLOGY TALENT WAR

## A Manager's Guide to Recruiting and Retaining Tech Workers in a Dot-Com World

# MARY ELLEN BRANTLEY

# CHRIS COLEMAN

**McGraw-Hill**

New York   San Francisco   Washington, D.C.   Auckland   Bogotá
Caracas   Lisbon   London   Madrid   Mexico City   Milan
Montreal   New Delhi   San Juan   Singapore
Sydney   Tokyo   Toronto

# McGraw-Hill

A Division of The **McGraw·Hill** Companies

1 2 3 4 5 6 7 8 9 0    DOC/DOC    0 9 8 7 6 5 4 3 2 1 0

ISBN 0-07-136474-9

This book was set in Janson Text by V&M Graphics.
Printed and bound by R. R. Donnelley & Sons Company.

This publication is designed to provide accurate and authoritative information in regard to the subject matter covered. It is sold with the understanding that the publisher is not engaged in rendering legal, accounting, or other professional service. If legal advice or other expert assistance is required, the services of a competent professional person should be sought.

*—From a declaration of principles jointly adopted by a committee of the American Bar Association and a committee of publishers.*

 This book is printed on recycled, acid-free paper containing a minimum of 50% recycled, de-inked fiber.

To

Jarrel Brantley, William Triggs,
Matthew Triggs, and Anne Anoff

and

John Coleman, Bridgitt Arnold,
and Alexandra Arnold

With Love and Gratitude

# Contents

## PART III

# Keeping Winners 163

# Acknowledgments

THANKS to Richard Narramore, our editor at McGraw-Hill, for his insightful comments. Richard, this is a far better book for your involvement. (Actually, it wouldn't even exist without your involvement, so double thanks.)

Thanks, too, to Jarrel Brantley and John Coleman, who tirelessly reread every chapter "just one more time," and to Elisabeth Mowris Deeter, who was instrumental in clarifying the idea for this book right from the beginning.

Our sincere appreciation to those who spent time with us for in-depth interviews. Their perspective gives this book both range and depth: Whit Blakeley, President & CEO CM Resources, Bridget O'Connor, Senior Vice President, Lehman Brothers; Kevin McGilloway, CIO & Managing Director, Lehman Brothers; Dexter Senft, Managing Director Fixed Income E-Commerce, Lehman Brothers; Bob Russell, Senior Vice President, Chief Operating Officer, Thomson Industries; Marriott Corporation: Carl Wilson, Senior Vice President, CIO, Kathleen Alexander, Senior Vice President, Information Resources/Human Resources, Stephanie Hampton, Manager of Communications, Information Resources; Ricky Steele, Director, Business Development, PriceWaterhouseCoopers, Robin Spangler, Senior Vice President, Computer Generation, Bob Lasher, President, Application Partners, Inc., David O. Ellis, Managing Director, EGL Holdings, Charlie Paparelli, CEO Paparelli Ventures, Inc.; Mike Strong, Director of Global Staffing, E*Trade Group, Inc.; Bennie Slone, Director MidSouth Area, Compaq Corporation Professional Services, Elaine Price, President & CEO, Phoenix Systems Integration, Phoenix Systems Integration GMBH, and CYA Technologies,

Inc.; Leland Strange, President & CEO, Intelligent Systems, Inc.; Jerry Gill, Director of Programs, Compaq Corporation; Miriam Pemberton, Consultant, The Thomas Group; D.W. Bracken, Ph.D., Psychometrician extraordinaire; Brent Thompson, President, Thompson Global Strategies International (TGSI), Kipp Jones, Vice President Technology, Video Networks, Inc, Kelly New, Vice President Chief Technical Officer, ECIndx, Chris Rouland, Director X-Force at Internet Security Systems, Dr. Anindya Datta, CEO, ChutneySystems, Regina Pontow, Abrams & Smith Publishing, Gail Oliver, President, Execume, Ben Carroccio, CEO OTEC.com, Tom O'Connor, Manager of Technical Recruiting, OTEC.com and Sgt. First Class James P. Beshada, New Jersey State Police Information Systems Department, Diane Costa, President, ThinkForce, Ben Hellming, Director of International Sales and Marketing, ITW Chemtronics, Carolyn Slocombe, Senior Human Resources Manager, Cisco Systems, Gus Scannapieco, CEO Optidoc.

Special thanks to Napolean Pinto, and Joanna V. Pomeranz of V&M Graphics for assistance in helping us edit this book.

# WINNING THE TECHNOLOGY TALENT WAR

# INTRODUCTION

# What Do Tech Workers Want Anyway? And Why Should You Care?

IF YOU LEAD a technology-driven company today, your ability to meet your growth objectives is most likely constrained by your inability to find the right technical people to take you where you want to go. A majority of technology companies are suffering from a tech talent shortage. The cost of this shortage is a bottom line issue that affects both today's business performance and the ability to pursue tomorrow's opportunities.

The situation won't get better anytime soon. The U.S. Department of Labor Bureau of Labor Statistics projects a 76 percent increase in demand for the total digital workforce by 2006. That's over a million new jobs that will be created in this sector alone. Computer scientists, computer engineers, and systems analysts represent the biggest job growth and will more than double within the same timeframe.

In an attempt to deal with this labor shortage, the Department of Commerce has initiated a project entitled "Bridging the Digital Divide." The emphasis of this strategy is to introduce more technology into schools and homes of every American, so that as children grow they may be attracted to the burgeoning opportunities in the technology industry. However, this strategy will require many years of implementation before we see the results in the workforce. In the meanwhile, the tech talent shortage will continue to grow.

### What can you expect from this book?

If you're responsible for recruiting or managing tech workers, the problem of finding qualified—or even almost-qualified—employees probably keeps you awake at night. In fact, it's likely that you have made some serious hiring mistakes simply because you were afraid nobody better would come along.

Relax. You *can* minimize downside risk and improve your employee retention rate. This book is for corporate managers and entrepreneurs who face the consequences of bad hiring decisions every day. It is also written for recruiters and consultants who advise their clients about hiring practices. For people on the opposite side of the fence—technical professionals considering a new job—here's a chance to see the world from a prospective employer's point of view.

This is not a theoretical treatise. It's a practical manual for business people in two situations: those with deep pockets and those with bare-bones budgets. The ideas for recruiting and re-training tech workers in each chapter can be scaled up or down depending upon your situation. Whether you're an entrepreneur with total control or a first-line supervisor with more responsibility than authority, you'll find useful advice on these pages that you can put to work immediately.

In this book you'll find out why the best-qualified professional may be the worst possible choice for your firm. You'll learn to see your company from a techie's point of view, and understand what it takes to differentiate yourself from dozens of other employers brandishing money and perks. You'll learn how to identify, interview, and hire IT professionals who work well with your existing team, and how to head off the politics and interpersonal conflicts that lead to employee turnover. You'll learn when and how *not* to hire: advice that can save you hundreds of thousands of dollars and untold misery. Finally, you'll see how other firms handle the challenges of growing and rewarding good tech talent.

You already know first-hand that winning the technology talent war is nothing like other business battles. Size, brute force, and lots of money won't guarantee victory.

What *does* succeed is asking a few tough questions (Does your company really have anything special to offer? If so, what is it? If not, what are you going to do about it?) and taking a hard look at the people you're hiring and why.

Finding and keeping good technology professionals takes time, resources, and commitment. You must master the fundamentals of finding and keeping winners. On these pages are the tools, techniques, and real-life experiences you need to do exactly that.

### Behind the research: interviews and survey techniques

While researching this book, we surveyed hundreds of tech workers and interviewed technology executives in a variety of industries. We were interested in three aspects of their experiences as employers and employees.

First, what role does the work itself play in a successful hiring scenario? Second, how much impact does the company culture or departmental culture have upon a candidate's interest in working there? And third, what constitutes management "leadership"— good *or* bad—and how does it affect recruiting and retention?

### Overview

Techies want the same thing everybody else does. Unlike many other workers, they have the luxury of holding out until they get it.

Quite simply, technology workers want meaningful work in an environment that lets them balance their professional and personal lives.

Pretty straightforward—until you factor in a million different definitions of the words "meaningful work" and "balance." That's where things get complicated. And that, of course, is real life.

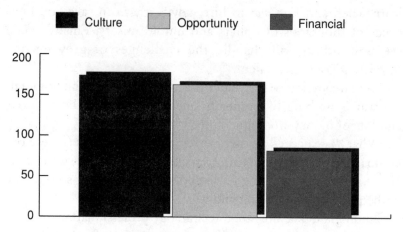

**Figure 1.1**   Reasons Tech Workers Join a Company

## "I'm looking for opportunity . . . but not just any opportunity."

According to research we conducted while writing this book, one of the primary reasons[1] technical people join a specific company is to exploit a particular opportunity: learn a new skill, perhaps, or deepen their experience in an area that will increase their market value. However, the opportunity in and of itself came in slightly behind the culture in overall importance.

## "I want to work for a company whose culture I admire."

*Which* opportunity they choose to accept is heavily influenced by the candidate's perception of the company's culture. This is the number one reason for selecting one organization over another. Culture infuses the vision and leadership of the firm, colors the challenges intrinsic to the job, and defines the work/life balance employees enjoy (or never have the opportunity to enjoy).

---

[1]33.4% said they joined a company for the opportunity. The combined opportunity scale is 36.6%. This includes the opportunity and job content.

## "I want money."

Compensation—salary, stock, and benefits—is third on the job seeker's priority list, trailing "opportunity" and "culture." Money matters, but it's not in first place.

*Least* important, according to our research, is "cool technology." Often considered a key factor in luring technical talent, many companies go to great lengths to provide the latest and greatest equipment. This is fine, but it's no substitute for what techies really want.

## What makes tech workers stick around?

When we asked IT workers why they stayed with their company after the honeymoon was over, we found some very different—but related—reasons.

The bar chart in Figure 1.2 shows their aggregated responses at a glance: culture, challenge, and compensation. Culture includes an environment where coworkers are respected and trusted, great leadership, and a place where the employee feels valued. Challenge includes the type of work an employee is asked to do, any training the employee receives to improve skills, and whether or not the employee perceives the work as having meaning. Compensation

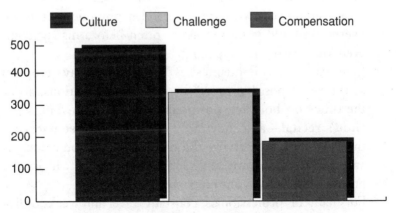

**Figure 1.2** Why Do Tech Workers Stay With a Company?

includes benefits and other types of renumeration. Respondents selected all the choices that applied to them.

### "I want to know my employer values me."

"Feeling valued" is the number one reason tech workers *stay* with an employer. This is important because it theoretically means that you can actually give your technical staff (and everybody else on the payroll, for that matter) what they want most *regardless* of your company or department's size, resources, budgets, or type of business. Plenty of firms talk about valuing their staff, but for many that's all it is: talk.

### "I want a life."

One of the most obvious clues to how much, or how little, a company values its people is to observe how it protects the balance between the staff's personal and professional lives. This balance manifests itself differently depending on the tech worker's perspective.

- The typical IT department is backlogged and understaffed, and in any struggle between the volume of work and the quality of the worker's life, the work usually wins. This means employees who are busy and happy one month are overworked and gone the next—often before management even knows what is happening.
- One axiom in this business is "problems always crop up at the worst possible time." People cancel vacations, go to the office on holidays, postpone birthday parties, miss the child's recital—and inevitably, a choice between serving the customer and serving the employee must be made. As an employer, the way you handle this conflict will have a profound effect on your employee retention rate.
- For many IT professionals, constant travel and weeks of living in hotels are a way of life. Extended periods of time away from home are stressful, particularly for workers with fami-

lies. Smart employers will look for ways to minimize time on the road.

There are no easy ways to do this, but Application Partners, a 40-person systems integrator in Atlanta whose employees have heavy travel requirements, takes an approach that has worked well for more than two years. Application Partners works a four-day week and actually turns down projects that would force its employees to violate this concept. The office is officially open Monday through Thursday, but it's not unusual to find employees there on Friday participating in training sessions or catching up on administrative work.

According to President Bob Lasher, "When we first put the four-day-week into place, it was a big draw because nobody else was doing it. Now, even the big boys offer it, but they haven't reduced the quota for billable hours. We have."

Some consulting firms offer tiered pricing as an incentive to clients to allow their project work to be done off-site. "Clients still generally expect their program manager to be on-site Monday through Friday," says Jerry Gill of Compaq's Professional Services Division. Over time, he adds, as rapport and trust develop between the customer and the program manager, "They realize work can be done through fax, phone, and e-mail and things ease up to a few days per week."

- For product development people, the pressure to perform is market-driven rather than client-driven. The challenge for software developers is to keep up the momentum while avoiding the pitfalls created by the nature of the work itself, much of which is tedious and repetitive. Since boredom is an ambitious young programmer's worst nightmare, the employer's challenge is to keep the work interesting without jeopardizing the product.

### "I want work that matters."

Right behind "feeling valued," the second most frequently cited reason for remaining with a company is the nature of the work

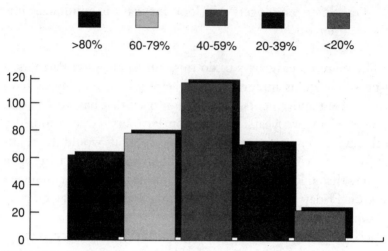

**Figure 1.3**   Percentage of Work That Is Creative vs. Tedious

itself. Our research revealed that people want their work to be meaningful. Repeatedly, they look for opportunities to do more than is asked of them, not less. The challenge for employers is to design work that accomplishes something, makes a difference, and allows people to contribute to the company in a meaningful way.

Building software is a creative exercise. Technology workers are restless people, always on the lookout for new opportunities to create, grow, and learn. This creates a dilemma: The more valuable a worker is in a given role, the more likely he or she is to get bored—and that's the beginning of the end. Keeping that hotshot on Project X for another year may increase your profit margins, but may also lead to an unwelcome vacancy on your IT staff.

It's interesting to note that 40 percent of our survey respondents describe 60 percent or more of their work content as "creative." Forty percent of respondents also say they're looking to make a job change. Is the correlation between low-creativity work and a willingness change jobs coincidental? Probably not.

### "I want to trust and respect the people I work with."

The third element that tech workers say bonds them to their employers is "trust and respect among coworkers." People simply want to work with those they trust. This refers not only to the character of the individuals, but to the collective character of the organization. A company that endorses doing the right thing— and supports employees who do the same—will prevail over opportunistic cultures.

Along these same lines, tech workers have little or no tolerance for corporate backbiting. Over and over, their write-in survey comments mention the importance of teamwork and their distaste for infighting and politics.

### Boiling it down . . .

Compensation, although important, is not the primary lure for technology professionals. People join—and stay with—firms that challenge them, excite them, and motivate them. Culture is important, but there's certainly no magic formula that appeals to everybody. The important thing is to be clear about what *your* company stands for, then search for individuals whose values and ambitions line up with yours.

PART
I

# Talent Hunting Tactics

# 1

# Think Like the Marketing Department! (It's Not as Scary as it Sounds.)

THERE WAS A TIME, not so long ago, when technical executives never said the word "marketing" without adding the word "fluff."

Those days are over. In a world where the IPO has become the ultimate marketing strategy, the best product on the planet doesn't stand a chance if it isn't marketed aggressively and well. Vacancies on your IT staff are no different.

Filling these positions calls for more than a fat address book and a good eye for talent. Recruiting and retention efforts that fail to incorporate four basic marketing principles simply don't stand a chance. *Nobody* will buy from you (that is, work for you) until you:

- get their attention,
- establish your credibility,
- prove the value of what you're offering, and
- ask for the sale in no uncertain terms.

This means your job is to promote your company or department, and the opportunities within it, as diligently as marketing people promote their brand. This doesn't have to cost a fortune, and you don't need a bevy of consultants to make it happen. You can put effective marketing and promotional techniques to work whether you're a line manager with little or no budget or a senior executive with plenty of resources. What you *do* need is imagination and persistence.

### What if nobody knows your name?

According to Mike Strong, director of global staffing at E\*Trade, "We have a backlog of applicants for every position, so we believe we can fill a job slot and get another person working within days of a turnover."

Lucky guy. How come E\*Trade can pick and choose while other companies are digging under rocks for talent? In a word: marketing.

The better known your company or department is beyond its own four walls, the easier it is to recruit good people. Certainly, it helps to be an e-commerce powerhouse with a multimillion-dollar advertising budget. But the issue here is one of scale, not approach. A five-person IT department in a small Midwestern town can apply the same principles that work well for the rich and famous.

Caveat: large corporations often resist renegade notions, and marketing an IT department falls into that category. "Market the *IT department?* Next thing you know the accounting people will want their own ad campaign! Forget it." Or, "We're promoting the company, not a bunch of separate entities. We can't dilute the brand." These are predictable responses, and to a certain extent, valid. But you *must* think boldly and act upon your ideas. Ordinary measures simply won't work.

If your company has a strong brand, is an industry leader, and understands the value of marketing, you're miles ahead. If you don't already have these advantages, employ as many of the tactics below as you can. It's easier to ask forgiveness than to ask permission, and you need all the help you can get.

### Refuse to be pigeonholed

You can't build a talent pipeline unless you get out of the office. Literally. Why? Because you need to see with your own eyes what's out there—and odds are good that your next IT hire already works at your company.

In the advertising business, 70 percent of new revenues come from an agency's existing client base, but most are so busy chasing prospects they never see the opportunities right in their own back yard. This principle, if not the percentage, applies to your situation.

*How can you do this if you're in a small company or a department with limited resources?* No matter how big, small, resource-rich or impoverished your situation, you can use this tactic successfully. Like so many marketing and networking techniques, it has nothing to do with money and everything to do with opening the lines of communication between you and the rest of the world. If you're out of the mainstream—if your department's housed away from other managers and influencers, or you work remotely—close the gap. Go where people are. Become visible, audible and recognizable, and *do this in person*, not through job posting boards or broadcast emails. People need to know first-hand that you're looking for talent. And remember, while you're sizing them up, they're doing the same with you.

### Move your fishhook

If you're constantly competing for talent (and losing) against bigger, better-known firms in your own city, find another fishing hole. This doesn't have to entail costly cross-country recruiting trips and relocation expenses. Focus on smaller cities a four-to-eight-hour drive away, where you'll uncover ambitious candidates who see your bigger-city location as a good career move.

Prepare well for these recruiting trips. Advertise in advance in the destination city (three newspaper ads spaced a week or so apart work well), and make this a fun, informal event. Rent a reception room, put on some music (no, don't rent a band), and serve snacks. The whole idea is to show people what your company has to offer in a casual, no-pressure setting, with the goal of scheduling follow-up interviews with qualified candidates at your site (and usually at your expense).

### How can you do this if you're in a small company or a department with limited resources?

Scale everything back. You can adapt aspects of this idea and still see results. Local libraries and schools offer free meeting rooms for community events, and letting a user group, trade association or civic organization know you're coming to town is an effective way to get the word out. If you encourage guests to bring friends and/or family you'll build critical mass—and convey your company's family-friendly corporate values at the same time.

### Show up in surprising places

In Seattle and San Francisco, the competition for IT talent is so fierce that employers and headhunters have become ingenious marketers simply to survive. They purchase ads on pizza boxes, pay restaurant owners to print their 24-hour employment hotline number on placemats, sponsor rock concerts and distribute promotional literature with the tickets ("Find your next great job at Bigbuck Systems!"), pay ski resort cab drivers a commission for every interview they schedule, and put recruiters on the beach in Panama City and Daytona during spring break. Far-fetched, yes; but brilliant guerilla tactics—and they make an indelible impression on the target audience.

### How can you do this if you're in a small company or a department with limited resources?

These techniques work because they're imaginative, not because they cost a lot of money. The magic word here is creativity. If you don't feel particularly creative yourself, pull together a group of coworkers for a brainstorming session. (These work best when they include participants from outside your own department.) Challenge yourselves to come up with 100 nontraditional ways to get the word out about openings at your firm. You'll leave the ses-

sion with at least 20 good ideas you can put to work immediately—guaranteed.

### Reward referrals

There's nothing new about this idea. Rewarding employees who
refer successful job candidates is standard procedure for most
forward-looking firms. If you're not doing it, better reconsider.
Variations on the theme, however, can make this practice even
more effective.

Most rewards are monetary, and $1000 bonuses (which go as
high as $10,000 at places like E*Trade) are pretty typical. But time
off is often more prized than money. Consider a hybrid incentive
for referring employees: a cash bonus plus a week off with pay.
Your department or company's situation will dictate which makes
more business sense.

Another effective twist on referral reward programs is to
include vendors and friends of the firm. Your suppliers have ongoing contact with a talent pool that you'll never reach as easily as
they can. Granted, you must think carefully here. You don't want
to put vendors in a compromising position with other clients
(nobody wants to buy from somebody who's raiding their staff),
and corporate policy prevents some from accepting referral fees.
It's sometimes possible to eliminate the latter problem by making
a donation in the vendor's name to the charity of their choice.

### How can you do this if you're in a small company or a department with limited resources?

Skip cash bonuses altogether and reward referrals exclusively with
time off. If you consistently run shorthanded, and your people
work long hours on a regular basis, the gift of time is priceless.
This could be the incentive that will make your referral network
explode. Don't be stingy here. A person's absence for a day, a
week, or even a couple of weeks will not bring your whole operation to a halt. (Think of it this way: If that employee quit tomorrow, you'd find a way to soldier on without him or her. You can
certainly do the same while they take a little R&R.)

### Make your recruiting and retention efforts newsworthy

Several years ago the Atlanta Business Chronicle wrote about a software company whose employee benefit package included company-leased BMWs for everybody. What seemed to be an incredibly extravagant gesture actually made financial sense, put the company front-and-center among potential employees, and spoke volumes about how serious the firm was about attracting and retaining talent.

You don't need to spring for BMWs across the board to catch the press's attention. The longer the talent shortage lasts, the more creative you'll become at finding and keeping good people, so don't keep your best ideas a secret. When you do something truly innovative, leverage it. Email or phone a business reporter and ask if he or she is interested in writing about it. (Do not send a press release. Ideas like these must be pitched one at a time.)

You may be thinking, "No way! We're not publicizing our secrets for the competition!"

Guess what? The competition knows what you're doing anyway—and if they don't, they'll certainly figure it out. With positive media coverage, you'll get exposure to potential employees you'd never reach any other way *and* earn public recognition as an innovator. This, of course, is exactly the attention you want.

### Publish an internal manifesto

What lights up your IT people? What do they stand for? Why do they stay? When the CIO of a Tulsa, Oklahoma, company faced the daunting task of hiring 700 (yes, you read that right: two zeroes) technical professionals within nine months for a massive reengineering project, one of the first things he did was produce a manifesto: a blunt, no-holds-barred document describing the culture he intended to build. When job applicants saw this, along with a companion document entitled, "Is this opportunity right for you?", they knew right way whether this was a place where they wanted to work. Here are the two documents:

## The Manifesto

*Our Creed*

Hire the best.
Expect the most.
Reward brilliance.

*Our Culture*

This is the next great billion-dollar company.
And we're in on the ground floor.

*Our Pace*

Make it succeed.
Then make it even better.
And do it now.

*Our Style*

We are not complacent.
We are not average.

*Our Challenge*

Build an information system second to none.
And while we're at it, we'll build a business legend.

## Is this opportunity right for you? It is if . . .

You wish you'd been in Redmond 15 years ago.

You know you're as good at your work as anybody,
anywhere—probably better—and you want to prove it.

You've got the edge and you want to keep it.

You can stand the heat.

You want to work with people quick enough to keep up with you.

You love to beat the competition.

You want to make money. Lots of it.

You want outstanding benefits, and you wonder what else
you can expect from a company with free day care.

You want to live somewhere you can still buy a lot of house
(maybe with a lot of land around it)
and not commute for hours to get there.

You want to live somewhere your family will love.
Where there's lots for families to do.

Beaverton. Redmond. Tulsa. You get the connection.

Not every organization is comfortable with this much attitude, but you'll find the more clearly you can express the character of your organization, and the more distinctive that character is, the more attractive you'll become to job seekers. Most important, you'll attract applicants whose values and drive match your own.

### How can you do this if you're in a small company or a department with limited resources?

Like so many of the other ideas in this chapter, this one costs absolutely nothing (unless you count the billable hours you and your people will spend writing the document.) This activity is particularly rewarding when done in a group, which is good news for managers who hate staring at a blank page hoping for inspiration.

### Find out where your staff hangs out

Sounds obvious, doesn't it? But it's amazing how few managers actually do this. What radio stations do your IT people listen to? What local papers do they read? Where do they buy pizza, CDs, coffee? Where do they grab a beer and rent their videos? Find out. These are ideal venues for the guerilla marketing tactics described earlier.

### What relationships can you develop with technical training firms?

Technical training is probably one of the twenty-first century's most cutthroat, competitive businesses. Hundreds of providers offer training for Microsoft, Oracle, Novell, Java, and Cisco certification, and they're all looking for a competitive edge to attract students.

Since those prospective students want better jobs the moment they earn their certification—and you've got jobs to fill—there's a natural connection here. Granted, these aren't necessarily highly skilled or experienced employees. And no, you can't guarantee a job, or even an interview, for most of them. But you *can* explore an arrangement with the training company that gives you the first look at each crop of graduates, no strings attached.

There are pitfalls in this scenario. No ethical training company will give you first crack at newly minted MCSEs whose certification was paid for by another employer. But career-changers and new entrants to the workforce are usually fair game, and when you see them first, you get first pick.

### Join trade associations and be an active member

No matter how small or how large your company or your department, this is one of the best ways to build a talent referral network. Simply joining won't do the trick, however. You must be an active, vocal, involved member to get your money's worth. Volunteering for a committee—marketing, community outreach or the job bank—delivers the quickest returns, but only if you follow through on all commitments you make. Oddly enough, doing a half-hearted job as a volunteer will often damage your reputation more than doing a half-hearted job you're paid for.

### Don't burn bridges, build them

Colleges and universities know that the secret to long-term success is simple: never lose touch with your alumni. It's an idea that business has been slow to adopt, but it makes consummate sense in a tight labor market. The concept is simple. Stay in contact with former employees and make them feel they still have a place in your organization. Send them your company newsletter, invite them to company parties, include them on the distribution list for press releases and announcements.

When job-hoppers discover the grass isn't greener elsewhere, many will ask to return if they know they will be welcomed. When they do, you won't find a more loyal worker. Experienced contributors who understand your culture and your business are invaluable. If and when they go, make sure they understand the door is still open.

### Repeat the message everywhere but the bathroom wall

Simple is always better. This particular trick is so easy, and so foolproof, that you'd use it even if you had a hundred qualified applicants for every opening. Just add a line to your email signature block that tells the world your company's a great place to work.

The wording can range from a direct call to action (Ask me about working with ABC) to something more subtle (ABC: the best place to build an IT career). The more people participate in this effort, the better it works. (You probably have staff members who won't clutter up their emails with a commercial message, but a generous referral bonus program usually overcomes most objections.)

### Follow up faithfully, and don't delegate this to HR

Companies that assume the relationship's over when they decide not to extend a job offer (or when the candidate turns the offer down) miss a huge marketing opportunity. Handled well, the relationship can actually be *strengthened* at this point to produce invaluable long-term benefits for both parties.

Think about the best and the worst job-hunting experiences you've ever had. Now imagine what the last person *you* interviewed is saying about your company right now. Glowing endorsement? Lukewarm? Downright negative?

Applicants in the first camp are superb advocates, and they're particularly credible because they're not even on the payroll. They refer friends and acquaintances, say good things spontaneously about your company and become influential ambassadors. It is impossible to calculate how much good—and how much damage—former candidates and applicants can do to your reputation as an employer.

Earning their goodwill is not difficult. All it takes is common courtesy, faithfully applied.

Send a handwritten follow-up note to everyone you interview. Yes, everyone. Yes, handwritten. And yes, *you* send *them* the note.

The underlying message is that you understand the value of the other person's time and appreciate their spending some of it with you. This is a powerful compliment and a gracious gesture few people will ever forget.

Apply this practice across the board: candidates you rejected, candidates who rejected you, and those who are undecided. *Do not assume someone else will handle this*, and don't delegate the task. There are few things more insulting than a fill-in-the-blanks thank-you letter.

### No recruiting brochure?
### Produce one now

Virtually every Fortune 100 company uses recruiting brochures, but they're scarce in smaller firms. That's too bad, because there's real value in a marketing piece targeted specifically to potential employees. The mere fact that it exists says, "Recruiting good people is so important to us that we make a special effort to tell our story professionally."

During interviews, individual managers tell your company story from their own perspective. They tend to forget key points; sometimes they leave out the anecdotes that emphasize your firm's unique personality. A well-written brochure guarantees that every applicant gets a consistent view of your firm.

Your recruiting brochure doesn't have to be an expensive four-color extravaganza. Keep it simple, keep it short, and keep it honest. Brief quotes from employees about why they chose to work here, a high-level description of your benefits package (a trump card few employers play to full effect), and a quick overview of your firm's industry, history and reason for being are the basics; everything beyond that is up to you. Don't gush and don't oversell.

If you're telling yourself you can get by without a recruiting brochure because (1) your corporate brochure does the trick; or (2) you expect applicants to get everything they need from your Web site, think again.

Making your corporate brochure do double-duty is like using the same business letter for every situation—it doesn't work for anybody but the sender. And don't expect the Web to completely replace ink-on-paper any time soon. Most applicants—even the most technically sophisticated—want something tangible to hold, fold, write on, and share with their families.

### How can you do this if you're in a small company or a department with limited resources?

Forget the graphic designer and copywriter. Sit down at your keyboard and make a list of your company's tangible benefits (health club membership, health insurance, family snow days) and intangible benefits (casual dress every day, walking distance to the park). Leave nothing out! Ask a few colleagues what they like best about working for your company, and capture their comments on paper. Print it all out on letterhead and put contact information in a visible place on every page. Simple as it is, you've produced something that 98 percent of your competitors don't have. Give it to everyone you interview and include it in your letter every time you acknowledge receiving a resumé. (You're responding to every resumé, remember?) Even prospects you turn down should know why your company's a great place to work. Odds are good they'll tell somebody else—who just might be your next superstar.

### Every teeshirt's a bulletin board

One of the most painless ways to make your company or IT department more visible is to sponsor a kids' soccer team, Corporate Challenge runners, a bowling league or a softball team. Thousands of techies abandon their computers every day to do something athletic, and they usually do it in public—at the gym, on the playing field or in the bleachers. Don't scoff at the impact a good-sized logo (with your URL, of course) can have on the back of a teeshirt. You'll never find a harder-working advertisement for under ten dollars.

### Make your Web site earn its keep

If you do nothing else, you must put time and effort into this. Eighty-seven percent of business-to-business buyers search the Web before they contact a company for product or service information, and informed job seekers behave the same way. They'll judge your firm based upon what they see on the Internet, so make sure the experience works in your favor. You'll find more about using the Web for marketing and communicating with candidates in Chapter 7.

CHAPTER

## 2

# Internet Recruiting

INTERNET RECRUITING was a novelty two short years ago, when only a handful of the world's biggest companies ventured online to attract workers. Today, 79 percent of those same firms use their corporate Web sites as recruiting tools. There are a whopping 29,000 job boards and 2.5 million resumés online, and 200,000 Web sites actively recruiting candidates.

There's no question that the Internet offers huge advantages to employers. Suppose for a moment that you're the HR director of a company bringing on three or four thousand new people a year. The sheer paper volume is enough to grind you right into the ground. (How many resumés must you sift through to net three thousand "keepers"?)

Now think what it would mean to slash by half the time it takes to fill a job, cut your cost-per-hire by nearly as much, and shovel mountains of paper into the recycling bin. That's exactly what happens when job seekers search an electronic job board (or your Web site) for the openings that interest them, then fill out an application online. Their information drops into a database, a search engine hunts for key attributes, and thousands of candidates are electronically narrowed down to a shortlist in moments rather than months.

It's important to point out that this is an ideal scenario, and real life doesn't always work this way. There are still piles of outdated electronic resumés on servers all over the world, and in most companies, harried HR people are still bailing as fast as they can. But to say recruiting on the Web is less expensive than the old-fashioned way is an understatement. Online recruiting can save thousands of dollars per hire, with lower administrative and advertising costs accounting for a huge hunk of the savings.

Posting job openings online costs a fraction of what corporations spend on classified newspaper advertising, yet the online version is visible for weeks while the hard-copy ad disappears in days. Turnaround time is dramatic, too. Instead of waiting a week to see your ads appear in the classifieds, you can post a position today and start getting resumés overnight.

Online recruiting in big corporations involves multiple elements, with three "musts" at the top of the list. These include full-time recruiters (in-house or hired guns) to mastermind the effort, online job boards, and the corporate Web site. Big-budget operations use media planners to sort through thousands of placement possibilities and recommend the best places to buy space (both online and traditional) for maximum visibility.

Even for companies with very deep pockets, the task is gargantuan. "Most recruiters feel overwhelmed by the degree of choice offered by the Web," according to the Electronic Recruiting Index. "It is humanly impossible for an individual recruiter to become usefully familiar with all the options."

That's one reason some firms simply rely on job board services as a turnkey resource for attracting, processing, and presenting candidates. Yet another alternative is to retain a third party to manage your site, process incoming resumés, and aggressively search for what the industry calls "passive" candidates—well-qualified people who aren't on the market, but could be persuaded to make a move for the right opportunity. Some professionals claim that these are the only people worth pursuing. ("Nobody visits job boards but the unemployed and the dissatisfied," sniffs one recruiter. "We're interested in a better-quality candidate.")

If you're an entrepreneur, small business owner or department manager without the resources for full-time headhunters or elaborate systems, you do have other options. A slew of companies offer packaged software and support for smaller enterprises to automate the recruiting process end-to-end. Interesting online services abound, too: one example is *www.recruiterscafe.com*, where both corporate and third party recruiters can post and review job openings, manage their applicant databases, screen candidates and share ideas.

One of the newest twists in online talent hunting is the Internet personnel auction. Called ludicrous by some and ingenious by others, these forums let IT professionals auction their services (as employees, consultants or independent contractors) to the highest bidder. At this writing not many auction sites are more than a year old, but it's an idea that's spreading. The business model is pretty simple: the site serves as intermediary between employee and employer, taking a flat fee (typically) for facilitating the negotiations.

No matter how you handle the logistics of online recruiting, targeting is the secret to success. You'll go nuts if you venture online without clear parameters for the type(s) of candidate you're looking for. Part II of this book tells how to decide which positions, skills, and personal attributes make most sense for your company. Make these decisions *before* you march into cyberspace.

Seasoned online recruiters use techniques that make them more productive and effective. Many share their secrets for a fee, either one-on-one or in seminars. If you're serious about talent hunting on the Internet (and if you're not, what's your alternative?) professional coaching will save you hours of frustration.

In the meantime, here are a few ideas to give you a head start.

*It's difficult to be a jack-of-all-trades.* Internet recruiting has two aspects: information-gathering and direct contact with the potential candidate. If you're hiring in volume, it's virtually impossible for one person to do both. If one person is all you have, be realistic. Research calls for one set of skills; candidate selection calls for another. Not many people are equally adept at both, and *nobody* has enough time to handle both well. (Now you know why professional recruiting is a growth industry.)

*Writing want ads for the Net is an art form.* "Every time I post something funny, I get a good response," says one software company owner. "Boring ads don't seem to work as well." Surprise, surprise. Boring ads don't work in the newspaper classifieds either, but that's never stopped anybody from writing them. Since you're not paying by the word on the Web, why not write something interesting?

- Candidates search job banks using keywords. If you're looking for Web designers but a likely prospect searches under "developer", the two of you may never meet. Plug in all the descriptors that apply (within reason) to boost your chances of being seen.
- The work environment matters almost as much as the work itself, so sell your culture. "Starbucks in the break room and beer every Friday." "Renovated warehouse, pets welcome."
- List the position's skill requirements in bulleted form so they're easy to scan.
- Include links to complementary sites that showcase the advantages of your company, your location or your business. Client and employee testimonials, community Web pages touting the advantages of your locale, and links to local universities are all good possibilities.

*Targeted newsgroups are a good place to hang out.* So are user groups and technology-specific chat rooms. Lurking and pouncing doesn't work, but establishing relationships does.

Read the newsgroup charter *first.* (No point in embarrassing yourself or blowing your credibility with an inappropriate post.) When you can add something of value to the conversation, pitch right in. Over time you'll get to know who's sharp, who's not, and when it makes sense to proceed one-on-one with an online correspondent.

"If you're looking for a strong Cisco person, go right to the Cisco site," advises Tom O'Connor, manager of technical recruiting for New York-based Otec.com. "They have chat rooms where somebody may say, 'I'm having this issue with my routing system; how do I fix it?' And somebody else will chime in with, 'Well, have you tried this or tried that?'

"So you jump in with 'I have a serious job opportunity in New York, do you know anybody?' Sometimes they'll be interested themselves, but they'll always refer their friends to you. Or they'll say, 'This company is using our product. There could be a candidate there.' Then you just get on the phone and do some cold calling. You'll get pointed in the right direction most of the time."

O'Connor also likes the WindowsNT site. "Once you get in there, start chatting, tell them you have a position that relates to what they're talking about, they get perked up," he says. "Sometimes I'll ask, 'How did you learn this?' and if they tell me, 'I worked with this great person,' I say I'd like to talk to that person. They may not be looking, but they'll always know somebody who is."

*Check out Operation Transition.* Too bad the U.S. military is so bad at marketing. On the other hand, maybe that's a good thing. If you're tired of fighting tooth and nail for seasoned talent, find out more about Operation Transition. This online bulletin board is easy to use, costs absolutely nothing, and hums along quietly connecting 24,000 employers with thousands of veterans coming out of the Armed Services each year. Run by the Department of Defense and the U.S. military, this database links employers with applicants—and 92 percent have technical skills of one type or another.

No search costs, no relocation costs (the military picks up the tab), and not much competition. At least one Fortune 50 employer is blunt about keeping the bulletin board quiet. "We wouldn't want to help other companies set up a program like ours," a spokesman told a reporter. "We feel we're recruiting people great people from the military and don't want to share them."

The secret's out. Go to *www.dmdc.osd.mil/ot/ot/* to find out more.

Need more ideas? These Web sites can spark your thinking and get you started.

- *www.recruiterscafe.com* Networking and placement site for recruiters and corporate hiring managers
- *www.netrecruiter.net* Seminars, sourcing services, and a chatty, interesting free newsletter called The Sourcerer's Apprentice

(click the "Resources" button for back issues and a sub-scription)

- *www.interbiznet.com* Publishes annual Electronic Recruit-ing Index and a free newsletter
- *www.tek-tips.com* Hundreds of focused, application-specific or function-specific forums for IT managers, programmers, trainers and Internet professionals.

One final caveat relating to Internet job posting and privacy: The jobs your company posts online are a clue to competitors about your business strategy and a neon sign for recruiters inter-ested in raiding your shop. From the employee's standpoint, there are few guarantees that the resumé he or she submitted to a job board months ago hasn't since been purloined, duplicated and reposted dozens of times. The individual never knows what hap-pened—until the boss, searching the Web for candidates, finds her employee right there with all the other job-hunters. Equally worrisome is the lack of protection for female applicants who worry about their contact information falling into the hands of a stalker.

Corporate directories, organization charts and employee in-formation are easy to snatch right off corporate Web sites if you've mastered the simple but time-consuming maneuver called site flipping. Don't know how? No time? No problem. Hire an online service to do it for you.

# CHAPTER

**3**

# Your Best Leads Come Through Networking

Yes, the cliché is true. It's not what you know; it's who you know—and who knows *you*—that counts.

Networking is the most effective way to find good people.

Candidates referred by a trusted source are nearly always better than those that come in over the transom. People filtered through your network come in with a more realistic impression of your company, and the person doing the recommending sends good people your way because his or her reputation is on the line. Your network is also the ideal place to refer qualified people who aren't suited to your organization—and the contacts you develop are priceless if you're ever job-hunting yourself.

If you picture networking as backslapping, good-old-boy stuff, think again. It simply boils down to visibility and cooperation, and you don't have to be a politician or a party animal to do it well. Developing this skill is essential if you're serious about managing, rather than simply reacting to, the talent scarcity.

*How do you get plugged in?* You're already in. If you're like most managers, you don't realize how well connected you are. Everyone you know—personally and professionally, directly or indirectly—is part of a huge web of contacts you've created over the years, an entire army of personal recruiters just waiting to be deployed.

This includes your family (immediate and extended), friends, neighbors, colleagues, former employers, teachers, professors and classmates (both yours and your kids'), professional associations, health clubs and church. Don't forget corporate vendors, that guy (or gal) who wants to sell you a new car, and your real estate and insurance agents. These people network for a living, so they are invaluable resources.

But until these people know what you're looking for, they can't send talent your way. Here are a few ways to mobilize your network.

*Friends and neighbors.* We can't emphasize enough that you *must* find a quick, clear, concise way to tell people what your company does. It's amazing how many technology professionals make no effort to help their families, friends and neighbors understand what they do. "My kids haven't got a clue what my job is all about," says the CIO of an Atlanta software services company. "It's so complicated I have a hard time even explaining it to other engineers."

Too bad. If he'd simply told his kids that he's responsible for building computer systems that catalog retailers like L.L. Bean use to take millions of telephone orders, his daughter undoubtedly would have mentioned it in passing to her best friend, whose father was an IT professional at MCI looking to make a move.

Keep in mind that when people ask what you do, it's like asking, "How are you today?" They *don't* want the details. Keep it short and sweet so they can connect you with other people they know who do similar work.

Develop your elevator speech! If you can't articulate in a sentence or two why your company's a great place to work, how will the people in your network do it? If you need some inspiration for this, ask a few recent hires what prompted them to join your firm.

*Coworkers and employees.* Go to *www.cisco.com*, click the "make friends @ Cisco" button, and you're face-to-face with an ingenious concept—the electronic version of an employee referral program. Click and you'll be contacted by an employee who answers all your questions about Cisco. Even people who aren't actively job-hunting get involved and next thing you know, they're filling out an application online.

Cisco's program is successful because it taps into human nature: people go where they feel welcome. This, of course, is the core of networking. Someone once said, "People don't quit their jobs, they quit their friends," and the same is true for people taking a new job.

Sixty-nine percent of the companies we surveyed say that employee referral is their most successful technique for attracting new workers. Multiply the number of people on your payroll by two or three hundred (roughly the size of each of their personal networks) and you'll see how huge the impact really is.

Nobody understands your corporate culture and what it takes to be successful better than people already on your payroll. They've made the decision to come to work for you, and they'd like their friends to join them. Since they are already motivated, financial rewards for referrals simply amplify their efforts.

Referral programs vary from company to company. E*Trade, for example, pays employees $10,000 for each successful hire. This is exceptionally high compared to even the most generous bonus programs, but E*Trade has a waiting list of qualified candidates and can fill a vacancy within a week. Is that due to the enormous bonus? Is it E*Trade's reputation, culture and working environment? Or is it a little of both? It's hard to say, but even if $10,000 a pop is too rich for your company to swallow, don't rule out cash incentives altogether. They work.

To ease cash flow and encourage retention, some companies are staggering bonus payments over a one-year period, paying 33 percent at time of hire, 33 percent six months later, and 34 percent at the end of the recruit's first year.

*Former employers.* Do you stay in touch with your old boss (es) and coworkers? If not, and assuming you haven't burned bridges, now's a good time to start. After all, who understands your management style better than the person who once hired you? Asking a former boss's opinion is a real compliment, and most will be happy to serve as talent-spotters because they know you'll return the favor.

*Teachers, professors, classmates.* If you don't belong to your college alumni association, join now. If you do belong but don't read the alumni magazine, start now. If you do read the magazine but don't pay any attention to the "milestones" section, turn to those pages first: they're loaded with good leads. Pay attention to who's working where, and figure out how they might be connected to talent pools you can't reach. When you discover that your former lab partner is vice president of lending operations at Bigbucks Bank and you need a programmer analyst with experience in financial applications, who're you gonna call?

*Your church, health club and professional affiliations.* If you've been lifting weights or singing in the choir with the same people for months but haven't mentioned the six-figure project manager slot that just opened up in your department, why not? Granted, many of us go to church and the gym to get away from the office, so bending somebody's ear indiscriminately is neither welcome nor productive. But don't rule out the help that's available to you from unexpected sources. If you don't ask, you don't get, and your next superstar could be on the treadmill right beside you.

*Company vendors and your personal service providers.* "The best employee I ever hired was referred by the woman who cuts my hair," says the head of product development at an Atlanta company. When the people you do business with, both personally and professionally, are aware that you're *always* on the lookout for good talent, your network expands exponentially. This is an extraordinarily powerful tool, and if your company's referral program extends to outsiders, a referral bonus is much appreciated (unless your contact's employer has a policy against it).

OK, now that you know who's in your network, here are a few creative ideas about how and where to look for talent. Remember: skilled networkers are always in recruit mode, and they're innately curious. The more questions you ask, the more you'll learn.

"People love to talk about themselves," says Whit Blakeley, president and CEO of CM Resources. "Ask them about themselves, their industry, their experiences." You'll uncover a wealth of valuable information and ideas. If you run across a good candidate or a person with access to good candidates, don't beat around the bush. Come right out and tell them about the position(s) you want to fill. Time is of the essence when you spot a potential winner.

Where are these potential winners, anyway? They're everywhere you'd expect—and in a few unexpected places as well.

*Trade associations, user groups and professional organizations* are the obvious starting point. If you're not a member of at least one industry-specific group, what are you waiting for? No, you *don't* have to glad-hand people at the door or volunteer for the membership committee (although it certainly couldn't hurt). You *do* have to go to meetings, talk to people, and make sure your firm is listed accurately in the membership directory. Since the whole point is to meet other people and to have them meet you, don't attend the first meeting and then find a dozen excuses why you can't make another one.

*Find out where your tax dollars are going.* The public sector funds scores of city, state and national training initiatives, many focused on developing workers with technical skills. Familiarize yourself with the funding cycles and services of these agencies. The employment and training division of the U.S. Department of Labor is implementing one-stop career centers in 33 states. These one-stops give employers and employees access to nearly a million national job listings, electronic resumé banks, labor market information, and a national training database. You're not likely to find a plethora of C++ gurus here. You *will* find motivated workers at all stages of their careers with recent training and documented qualifications. For more information and a directory of contacts, go to the Training Technology Research Center Web site: *www.ttrcnew.ttrc.doleta.gov/common/directories.*

D.C. Link & Learn is a joint initiative between blue chip firms like Microsoft, IBM and Novell and the Federal government. This three-year-old program gives lower-income people the skills they need for IT careers. Participants are trained in network systems, software development, multimedia and geographic information systems.

*Broaden your definition of "talent pool."* There's a wealth of untapped potential on the periphery of the Internet economy. Some of these people require an investment in time or training, others are ready to roll: all they need is a way into the system.

Underrepresented in the U.S. technical ranks are African-Americans, Hispanics, women, senior citizens, and disabled workers. Industry observers have raised a provocative issue: if these groups were recruited in force, would there even *be* a tech labor shortage? Although the question is academic at this point, the opportunity isn't. The Association of Mexican Professionals in Silicon Valley, the Black Data Processing Association (BDPA)

*(You will find a BDPA chapter on the Internet for most locations. For more information go to http://www.bdpa.org)*, Women In Technology International (WITI), the Peninsula Association of Black Personnel Administrators in Sunnyvale, CA, and other special-interest groups are direct conduits to under-recruited technology talent.

*Join forces with other companies.* It's hard to make a splash when you're a small company competing against the "bigs," but teaming with other firms can create momentum that will help you reach more candidates. The Japanese notion of "kieretsu"—which has no direct English translation, but is roughly equivalent to a network of companies with shared interests—applies here. Eighteen tech firms in Fairfax, VA, put the concept to work by banding together with a local radio station and a recruiting firm to host a mini-job fair at Fast Eddie's Billiard Café. Guests needed nothing more than two years of IT experience, a resumé and proof that they were 21 to get in the door, where they played free pool all night and drank complimentary beer from 9:00 until 10:00 p.m.

The best recruiting parties are low-key, informal and fun. And they need critical mass to be successful, so when you and your co-hosts put together the guest list, don't forget to invite your own employees.

*Jump the fence.* Corporations employ nine IT-related people for every one IT professional at a tech firm. That means software and Internet companies have a pool of about nine million heads to hunt, compared to the million in their own back yard. (This figure doesn't include technology professionals at government entities, non-profits and small entrepreneurial companies.)

The technology industry has a tendency to dismiss "corporate types," as hidebound, old-economy folks who just don't move fast enough. One seasoned CIO says, "Too many people who come out of the big shops sit in the same corner and monitor the same system year after year, so they don't learn anything."

There's some truth to this, but on the whole it's a gross generalization. And let's face it: who can afford stereotypes in a labor market like this? If you're stubbornly clinging to the notion that a candidate's experience must perfectly match the job description, maybe it's time to reconsider.

On the flip side, corporate positions are looking better and better to technologists who have lost their taste for the wildly unpredictable dot.com world. If you're a manager on the user side, the climate's right to go after techies in entrepreneurial firms, consultants weary of life on the road, and professionals in smaller cities who want to move upmarket—or vice versa.

Many technology firms are founded and run by cadres of B-school classmates or tech teams that once worked together at a bigger firm. For entrée to these companies, look for college alumni association contacts. (There may be some on your own payroll.) Many larger firms, including the former Digital Equipment Corporation, spawn "alumni" clubs of former employees.

What makes a network keep working? Reliability and reciprocity. Stick to these principles and in time you'll be two to four phone calls away from all the information, resources and help you'll ever need—anywhere in the world.

### Reliability

- Follow up and follow through without fail.
- Never, never badmouth your firm, your product, your employees, your coworkers or your competitors. Derogatory comments will *always* come back to haunt you.
- Raiding doesn't work. It can jeopardize your network relationships, and you'll pay for it sooner or later. Take non-compete agreements seriously.

### Reciprocity

- Networking is a two-way activity. Contribute information as well as ask for it, and your network will grow exponentially.
- Never succumb to the notion that you've got nothing to offer. You *always* have information that's useful to someone else.
- By definition, your network includes your competitors. Speak well of them when it's justified and they'll hear about it. Maybe they'll even reciprocate.

# Techniques for Attracting Superstars

Hiring a superstar is like making sourdough French bread. Nothing happens without the starter—that yeasty stuff that makes the whole loaf rise.

Bakers get starter in one of two ways: from another baker, or (if they're patient) by making it themselves. The latter is a tricky process involving a delicate interplay of temperature and chemistry, and frankly, not everybody has the knack or the time to do it right. So if you're in a hurry, it makes sense to pay for a fresh-baked loaf and enjoy the results of somebody else's efforts.

All of this is to say that the hardest part of building a stable of superstars is getting your hands on the starter. Once the first one's in the door, others follow. Talent attracts talent. Exceptionally talented people go where they are recognized, appreciated, challenged, rewarded—and have other talented people to hang around with.

Keep one point in mind: never try to fill your ranks entirely with superstars. Team dynamics fall apart when they play every position. Obviously, you need *top performers* in every role—but *not* all top performers are superstars. Superstars tend to be heavy hitters. Their impact is very powerful and they will exert a strong influence on any department, division, or group they are involved with, so select them with care.

What *is* a superstar, anyway? We define it first in terms of reputation, then charisma and leadership. People who are recognized by their peers as having all these in abundance (accompanied, of course, by exceptional skills and talent) are what we're calling superstars. Superstars tend to come in a two varieties:

- The technical genius whose reputation precedes him or her. They may be technically deep (a Guru) or wide (a Sherlock) and possess superb critical thinking skills that can be applied across multiple technologies.
- The multi-talented individual who is strong both technically and interpersonally. This superstar has strong leadership capability.

The Superstar is an aggressive learner, a quick study who can rapidly sift through conflicting, often ambiguous information and make a decision. He or she drives organization learning and raises the competence level of the entire group.

The Superstar is a problem solver who can make decisions amid uncertainty.

Superstars are performance driven. They will coax cajole, and persist until goals are achieved. They tend to be optimistic, and can stabilize an organization that is in chaos.

Superstars get along well with others. Effective and powerful communicators, they exert great influence over others.

True superstars are people of integrity and character. There are plenty of talented people with deficits in both those areas. Don't let a stellar resumé distract you from due diligence in the hiring process.

Compatibility with your corporate values is vitally important when bringing on high-profile players. Superstars will influence your staff, your product, your customers, and your entire company... for better or for worse.

Every high-achiever asks himself or herself three questions when faced with a new job opportunity. First, *How fast and how much will this help me advance?* Second, *How will this help me live my life the way I want to live it?* And third, *What are you willing to do to get me?* This last includes, but isn't limited to, compensation. Superstars know they're in demand. They want to be sure *you* know it. (This is not necessarily a bad thing. It's just a fact.)

When you're recruiting a superstar, you're being interviewed too. Prepare as you would for an important sales call, because like it or not, you're selling. Your job is to describe clearly and convincingly what your department or company has to offer. *Enthusiasm counts.* If you're not genuinely excited about the opportunity you're presenting, the candidate won't be either.

Ben Carroccio, CEO of Otec.com, has a reputation for being able to snag superstars for his clients. By the time Carroccio has made his first contact with the target, he already knows everything about him or her—work habits, motivators, where they went to school, hobbies, where they go to church. He has more than likely been tracking the individual's career for several years before making the first contact.

Carroccio attributes his success to superb research.

> "It's like having only one pitch to strike the person out with, so you had better be prepared before you call," he says. "You have to be different than the ten or twenty recruiters that contact these people every week."

This is worth repeating. Superstars have plenty of options before them, so your own passion and energy are crucial to the success of your recruiting effort. If you find you're consistently failing to close highly desirable candidates, ask yourself a few questions, and answer them honestly. How committed are you to your job? Are you excited about the work your department and your company are doing? Most important, do you *really* want a superstar on staff? Hiring a heavy hitter can be threatening, and ambivalence is difficult (some say impossible) to disguise.

*How can you identify a superstar?* By definition, they stand out. This does *not* mean they're outgoing or particularly well networked or flamboyant. Quite the opposite may be true, in fact. But colleagues in their area of expertise always recognize them. If you ask several people, "Who's the best project manager you know?" and the same name keeps popping up, it's likely you've identified a superstar.

Superstars as a group are highly intelligent. Some are highly intelligent and narrowly focused. Those in the latter category are often superstars-in-the-works: "C" students in areas they care nothing about, but channel them in the right direction and watch the electricity.

Kevin McGilloway, Managing Director and CIO at Lehman Brothers in New York, slots employees into quintiles within 24 months on the job. For those in the top tier, the company tries to eliminate financial consideration as a variable, paying people in the upper three quintiles at 120 percent or 125 percent of market.

"Philosophically, we believe that if you can keep a high retention rate in your top 10 percent and acceptable but low (turnover) in your next 30 percent, that's the core talent base for building your leadership," McGilloway says, "You have to target so the losses stay in quintile four and five. If it shifts into one and two, you're dead."

*Grunt work won't work.* Superstars aren't cut out for it, and it's a waste of their talent. Some flatly refuse to do it; others do it so poorly you wish they'd just said "no" to begin with. This is infuriating for coworkers and executives who believe that everybody *must* come up the hard way, so prepare for a backlash. Older workers may resent young hotshots coming in and not "paying their dues." But getting rid of that attitude is the price your team must pay if you want to attract and keep superstars. "Successful companies give them challenging work and involve them immediately in decision-making opportunities," says Ralph Mobley, director of career services at Georgia Institute of Technology at Georgia Tech. Involve your hotshots in special projects, give them lots of exposure, but use coaching as a safety net to assure that they don't make costly mistakes.

Look at it this way. You're hiring a superstar—current or potential—not for a specific job, but for the ability to contribute to the overall success of your organization. Resist plugging stars into a niche: if it's too confining, it won't hold them for long.

*Money counts. More money counts even more.* At least one industry observer claims that high achievers deliver up to one hundred times more value than the average worker does. This means pay differentials for superstars are here to stay. Roughly half the top-performing companies surveyed in 1999 by Towers Perrin give their best producers pay increases one to two times greater than that of the average employee; 13 percent give their best people at least two to three times more.

Annual pay raises are simply too far apart for today's electronic marketplace. Superstars aren't interested in twentieth-century compensation packages; they're looking for a significant upside, both in terms of equity and performance-based pay. Venture capitalists, who are often in the role of corralling superstars, tie equity to performance and tenure to hold onto talent.

If the idea of shelling out more and more money annoys you, maybe a few statistics will help put this into context. Wages rose an average of 27 percent from 1991 through 1999. During the same period, corporate profits increased 105 percent, the average CEO's compensation went up 163 percent, and the Standard & Poor 500 jumped 218 percent.

*Never underestimate the power of bragging rights.* Superstars are almost obsessive about their professional reputations, and they're attracted to situations that let them polish that reputation even more. They earn bragging rights when given the chance to do something nobody else has been able to accomplish. Your superstar needs to feel that the work she's doing is important and will lead to something bigger. Give them enough room to stretch and grow.

Even the most challenging work in the world won't hold high achievers if they're surrounded by underperformers, however. Superstars hate the idea of working anyplace that tolerates mediocrity. They'll expect you, as the manager, to help marginal players get better—or get out.

*Once you've got them, how do you keep them?* Here's a chat room comment that sums it up nicely: "Ninety-nine percent of software engineers think they're smarter than their boss. Ninety percent are right. So ask their advice, let them set deadlines, act as a shield from the crap above, and foster an atmosphere where success is applauded and failure's a one-off event."

*They want access to the top.* How willingly do you listen to new ideas and suggestions for improvement? Most managers give themselves pretty high marks, but their employees don't always agree. This discrepancy has been documented time after time, so don't make assumptions. Find out where you stand and make improvements where you need to.

*Superstars resist bureaucratic and cultural control.* If you're going to manage superstars successfully, you must focus less on *how* employees get their jobs done and more on *what* they actually produce. Fewer and fewer stellar employees are willing to sacrifice their lives for their work. Flex time, telecommuting, job-sharing and childcare accommodations are more important than ever, and more companies offer them.

Sadly, though, there's plenty of evidence to suggest that managers actually reward people who *don't* use these options. One eye-opening Gallup poll indicates that 41 percent of employees working for companies with family-friendly policies believe that using the benefits would harm their careers.

Warning! If you pay lip service to work/life balance but the reality is different, you'll have a hard time hanging on to your best people. Early-morning, late-evening and weekend meetings are just one of the not-so-subtle ways to say, "your job comes first, last and always."

A fascinating excerpt from a study conducted by Leslie Perlow, University of Michigan Business School, points out the pervasiveness of the notion that "if you're not here, you're not working."

"One female engineer tried to create an alternative way of working so that she could limit her hours and still meet her work demands. Six months before I arrived, she was a project team leader. She created a rotating position such that one day a week one of her engineers would fill in for her. This enabled her to work at home on this day, saving two and one-half hours of commuting and providing her with uninterrupted time in which to work. Moreover, her group members each had the unusual opportunity to act as project team leader while she was at home. As a result, they developed managerial skills, and the project did not suffer. Her six-month performance review noted that her group was on schedule. Her managers, however, never acknowledged her innovation. Instead, just before I arrived, she was reassigned to a position as an engineer working with confidential data that could not leave the lab. She could no longer work from home."

"One of the male engineers worked Saturdays instead of Mondays in an attempt to accommodate his own ambition and his wife's expectation that he be home at night. Another engineer worked from home one day a week to balance work, a long commute to work, and family responsibilities. Frustration led each of them to create new ways of working that enabled them to do the same work, or sometimes even more, in constrained amounts of time, but none of them benefited from these efforts in terms of career progress. Moreover, each received little or no increase in pay."

*Two skills that high achievers think they need to master.* Superstars want an environment where they can fine-tune management capabilities that they can't easily assimilate on their own. The areas they're most interested in improving are leadership and communication, and they jump at the opportunity to work with someone who can teach them those skills.

*Where can you find superstars?* Hanging out with other superstars. If you don't have an employee referral program in place (is there a company left in America that doesn't?) start one now. Go to tech conferences and pay particular attention to the people pitching innovations and giving papers. Start a relationship. Begin now to build the rapport that may attract him or her to your firm. And while you're at it, develop a relationship with a good recruiter. They're paid to know where hot talent hides out.

*What have you got right under your nose?* It's easy to spot superstars outside the gate. How good are you at recognizing the ones right under your nose? Sometimes you don't see them at all until they're hired away at twice the salary—and suddenly they look awfully appealing.

Sooner or later your best and brightest probably *will* move on—either to more responsibility in your firm or to your competitor's. The genius behind the development of VMS for Digital Equipment Corporation left to find greater challenge, ultimately becoming the genius behind Windows NT for Microsoft. There's always another star on the horizon, and your job is simply to provide a place to shine. This chat room comment sums it up pretty well:

"Ultimately, all the nap rooms, potato chips, stuffed animals and beanbag chairs managers use to attract talent mean nothing compared to the recognition you get for a meaningful, positive contribution.

"That recognition means interesting new job offers, networking with the nicest and best programmers in the world, and (of course) mucho dinero."

# CHAPTER

## 5

# Campus Recruiting

B EFORE YOU SET foot on campus, be forewarned: college recruits are a tough crowd. Twenty-seven percent of them actually figure they'll be millionaires by the time they're 30. That, at least, is the result of an informal Web poll conducted by recruitment site jobtrak.com in early 2000. (But wait, there's more. A full 53 percent of the respondents expect to hit the magic number before they're 40.)

Clearly, colleges are no place to try your sales pitch for the first time. "Students can smell B.S. a mile away," says Ralph Mobley, director of career services at Georgia Institute of Technology. "You just can't snow them, and to try is ridiculous. They're pretty clear on what they want and what they plan to accomplish in a certain period of time, and they expect the company they work for to provide that opportunity."

Your job is to demonstrate exactly how your firm can do that. Forget the brochures with full-color pictures of your board. Students respond to real people, and a smart, charismatic ambassador will do more for your company's image than anything else will.

It's important to send the A team. "If you want to get top people off the campuses, you've got to get your top people *onto* the campuses," says Kevin McGilloway of Lehman Brothers. Well-meaning but technically shallow representatives can't hold their own when students ask hard questions—and they will—about your company's technology strategy, technical resources and competitive stance. You'd better have an informed line manager on hand who can answer crisply and accurately.

The do's and don'ts of campus recruiting are pretty straightforward. You don't need a big budget, legions of representatives or gimmicks to do it effectively. But there *are* magic words with universal appeal to students, and the more of these claims you can honestly make, the better. This is what motivates them as they look for their first job.

*"Come learn from us. We'll mentor you."* Students crave decision-making responsibility, exposure to senior management, and the opportunity to learn as much as they can as fast as they can. They'll want to know if you offer rotating work assignments and ongoing scheduled training. A formal mentoring program is a huge selling point, but don't promote it if your company gives it lip service rather than real support.

*"Work/life balance really means something at our company."* We've heard about those college students who plan to be millionaires before they're 40. Now here's another survey, where 45 percent of the respondents say "being able to have a rewarding life outside work" is the most important factor in selecting their first job.

Hmm. Somebody's in for a surprise.

Plenty of young people entering the workforce want it all. Everything. Lots and lots of money and lots of time to enjoy it. Realistic? No. But if you offer flexible hours, telecommuting, job sharing, sabbaticals after time in-service, and family-friendly leave policies, you're way ahead of more rigid employers.

*"People love it here. There's always something going on."* Energy and action—both inside and outside the company—are irresistible to recruits. The current hotspots on college students' radar screens are Austin, the Bay area, Boston, New York and Seattle. Why? Because there's plenty to do. This doesn't mean you're completely out of luck if you're in Tulsa or Spokane. Focus on the attributes your community *does* offer, and put extra effort into revitalizing the atmosphere inside your own four walls. Somber co-workers, quiet halls, and a measured pace are anathema to college recruits. If your corporate culture can't adapt, look for talent somewhere else.

*"You'll make a difference here."* There's not much challenge in maintaining a system, a process or a product. College kids (like most motivated workers) get charged up about *creating* something. Nobody wants to be a faceless, nameless number. If a student's interviewing for a slot on a project team in a 40,000-person company, explain how the team fits into the department and how the department impacts the company.

*"We understand and value technology."* No matter what your business, you must be enthusiastic about your technology when recruiting. Don't pretend you're a bleeding-edge IT shop if your company's powered by green-screen AS/400s. But whether you manufacture lumber or human genomes, it's imperative to emphasize the role, and the importance, of technology in your company's overall strategy.

*"Our culture's wide open. Forget politics."* Students want to know that anybody who shares your company's values and beliefs will fit in, regardless of race, gender, sexual orientation or age.

*"Yes, we pay signing bonuses."* OK, here it is—the inevitable conversation about money. In 2000, the average starting salary for electrical and computer engineers with a BS degree topped $50,000 for the first time, with signing bonuses ranging from $2,000 on up. There are bizarre exceptions, of course, like the Texas company that offered a BMW 323ci as a signing bonus for an entry-level position paying $200,000.

*"You'll have a decision within the week."* You must move fast or you'll be branded as hopelessly bureaucratic. EDS Corp. has slashed its interview-hiring process to five days. A specially outfitted Winnebago—with computers, TVs, satellite backups, a GPS system and interview rooms—travels to campuses, where a 30-person campus relations crew meets with students.

No Winnebago? No problem. Just streamline your recruiting process. Sluggish decision-making is the mark of a sluggish company, and nobody wants to work for a slug. Besides, if you wait too long to extend an offer, the candidates you want will be taken.

Now that you know what works, here are a few tips on what to avoid. These "don'ts" will protect you from most campus recruiting pitfalls.

*Don't put your eggs in a few gold-plated baskets.* If you think only certain schools are worthy of your attention, think again. The top ten MBA programs for IT managers are nowhere near the Ivy League. Schools turning out the most heavily recruited technology graduates include Northeastern University, University of Texas, University of Maryland, University of Alabama, Southwest Missouri State University and the University of Florida.

*Don't be discouraged about your acceptance levels.* Fifty percent is about the going rate.

*Don't try to get away with paying bottom dollar.* This market won't allow it. You'll either pay up front, in the form of salaries and benefits, or you'll pay the other way—through attrition, turnover and extra recruiting, training and startup costs.

*Don't schedule recruiting events before checking campus calendars.* When a recruiter from a software company in Washington, DC, held an information session at Georgia Tech one Halloween night, "the only two geeks on campus who weren't invited to a party came," says Ralph Mobley. "Maybe she did have a tight schedule, but in my opinion it was a waste of money."

*Don't leave phone messages for students.* "They don't return phone calls, but they do read and respond to email," says Mobley. They need to respond on their own terms. They may not be there to pick up the phone, but if they're checking email at 2:00 a.m. they can get back to you.

*Don't focus on resumé-collecting.* Focus on building a relationship. Not a deep one, obviously, but something less superficial than "fill out this application and we'll get back to you." You'll have to spend enough time on campus to get to know people on a first-name basis.

This isn't as difficult as it may sound. Target the students you're interested in and the groups they belong to. Attend IEEE chapter meetings, for example, if you're going after electrical engineers, or the Association for Computing Machinery (ACM) for computer science majors. Host a reception or ask to make a presentation. Be visible.

Learn all you can about student life, clubs, academic programs and departments, hangouts, and associations. If you can't devote someone full-time to this, enlist the people in your company who know the market better than anybody: recent graduates.

On-campus interviewing is just the first step in successful recruiting. Close rates jump dramatically when you get students onto your own turf, and this is doubly true if your company isn't glamorous or well known.

When candidates see and talk to people on the job and experience first-hand what your workplace is like, they get excited. Introduce them to a few enthusiastic employees and let the chemistry go to work.

Don't overlook the power of a good internship program. When managed well, it's probably the best campus relations tool you could hope for. Returning interns are dyed-in-the-wool campus ambassadors for your company. The opposite is true, too, so don't offer internships or co-op programs until you have the bandwidth to make them truly valuable for the student.

At the University of Maryland, local businesses team up to give mid-Atlantic college students real-world IT experience. The "IT for the New Millennium" initiative is open to students from 13 Maryland colleges and universities, who attend a five-week technical training course paid for by the University. Participating companies then reimburse the university when a student signs on for an internship.

The interns agree—via written contract—that they'll stay for a specified time, while employers agree to pay one year of tuition toward an IT degree for every six months the intern works. Interns are also paid $15 an hour and attend school part-time while holding down their full-time job. (Employees who break the contract forfeit all tuition dollars.)

As you plan your recruiting strategy, remember that the best programs go beyond the students. Recruit the faculty, too. Nobody on campus has a better perspective on the superstars, the have-potential-but-haven't-found-themselves yet, and the duds.

How do you reach faculty members? Start with the career services department. "All it takes is a few phone calls or a few emails, some grunt work and a little assertiveness," says Ralph Mobley. "Once you know one person, it's just like any other networking...ask who else you should talk to."

Jerome A. Katz has compiled a list of nearly 300 business and entrepreneurship professors who are available for business consulting, and these people can also steer you in the right direction on campus. Go to *www.slu.edu/eweb/chair.htm* to download the list.

Finally, keep in mind that your company is a resource for local universities. Collegiate advisory counsels are hungry for corporate members, and getting involved has real benefits for both sides. You'll raise your firm's visibility on campus, and you may actually have the opportunity to shape what your future employees learn.

# 6

# What You Need to Know About Working with Headhunters and In-House Recruiters

HEADHUNTERS ARE PAID to find candidates you can't find on your own. They are *not* paid to guarantee the success of those candidates. That's hard to swallow when you've just spent thousands on a retained search that turned up dry, or a senior programmer who bailed after six months. But the responsibility for defining the position and making the final choice rests squarely with you, the hiring manager. Do your homework before you pick up the phone.

"Do your homework" means two things. First, figure out what type of recruiter will serve you best; second, be very clear about the talent you want that recruiter to find. "Sixteen C++ programmers with two years of experience" won't cut it. Once a good recruiter understands how your organization works functionally and politically, and knows what you're looking for in a candidate, he or she can uncover people to literally propel your company to the next level.

Nothing productive happens, however, without a staffing plan. In Part Two you'll see how to put together a staffing plan, so if you decide to skip ahead and come back, go right ahead. Just don't talk to a recruiter until you've got that plan in hand. Without it you're both flying blind.

This chapter talks about both on-staff and outside recruiting. Companies hiring in any volume usually bring the recruiting function in-house to control costs (which doesn't always happen), then tap job boards, retained or contingency search consultants, and independent contractors to round out their staff capabilities or handle special projects.

Smaller firms experiment with anything and everything (or nothing at all) when it comes to professional recruiting, modifying the mix until they get a formula that works. Whatever your approach, there's one universal truth: good recruiters are treasures, and bad ones can seriously damage your business.

A headhunter's networks and skills tend to focus on talent within a certain compensation range, with natural divisions at roughly three points: $60K, $150K, and $300K+. Good ones can recruit up and down several levels, certainly, but you probably wouldn't use the same person to source project managers and your chief technology officer. Here's a rundown on the types of service available:

*Retained Search Consultants*—These firms work on an exclusive basis (similar to law firms) and target candidates earning at least six figures. They charge either a flat fee or a percentage of the candidate's total first-year compensation, and the best ones combine all the best qualities of a management consultant and a shrink. Fee percentages range from 10 percent to 33 percent, usually due in three installments: one when the contract is signed, another when a shortlist of candidates is presented, and the balance when the candidate is hired.

Fee structures in this sector are in turmoil, however, and the traditional 33 percent is on the way out. Inquire about discounts for multiple searches, flat-fee arrangements, or paying a combined flat fee/percentage rate. And don't be surprised if your consultant requests stock or equity in lieu of—or in addition to—a fee.

You'll find contact information for qualified retained search firms in the *Directory of Executive Recruiters* (Kennedy Publications). Another resource is the Association of Executive Search Consultants at *www.aesc.org*.

*Contingency Search Consultants*—Contingency recruiters are paid only if you hire one of their candidates. Although they'd prefer you list your search with them exclusively, that seldom happens. These firms specialize in two types of talent: administrative (usually at the $60,000 salary level or below) and professional/technical, where candidates typically make between $50,00 and $80,000 a year. Volume is the key to profitability for contingency search professionals, so for economies of scale they often specialize in a specific niche. Beware of generalists: their networks may not be deep enough in the tech sector to include the contacts you need. The National Association of Personnel Services in Alexandria, VA, publishes a directory of industry-certified professionals.

*"Con-tainer"Hybrid Consultants*—This approach is an effort to combine the best of both retained and contingency searches: the concentrated attention you receive from a retained firm, but for a lower fee. There's a nonrefundable up-front charge (anywhere from $2500 to $7000), then a reduced percentage of the candidate's first-year earnings (typically 15 percent to 18 percent) due upon hiring.

*Web Recruiters*—Blue-chip traditional search firms and mass-market job boards are meeting on the Web, and the collision's had an effect on both. In theory, Web recruiters' prices correlate to the level of personal service they deliver and the quality of their candidate database.

PeopleScape, the online arm of Christian & Timbers (which placed CEO Carly Fiorina at Hewlett-Packard), launches online executive searches for $10,000 and up, and FutureStep, the Korn Ferry/Wall Street Journal venture, does the same. At the other end of the spectrum is CareerMosiac.com, where you can search a gargantuan database for $999 a year and post job openings for less than $200.

*Unbundled Services*—This is the pay-as-you-go approach, where the firm works on an hourly basis researching, qualifying and interviewing candidates or performing reference checks. If you have limited resources in-house but need professional help in specific areas, this may be a good bet. A directory of firms offering unbundled services is available from The Recruiting and Research Report, (800)-634-4548.

The recruiting industry has a terrible reputation. Sharks, vultures, body-snatchers—they're out there in full force. What separates great headhunters from the rest of the pack? Ethics, passion, perseverance, business sense, and a first-class network. Due diligence on your part can uncover most of those qualities (or lack thereof).

Don't hire headhunters without checking references. "Talk to people they've placed and see how they treat candidates," says Tim Barton, president of Barton Executive Search in Atlanta. "Does he or she really represent what your company stands for?"

Some recruiters are successful in spite of themselves: arrogant, rude, self-centered and obnoxious—but boy, can they fill those positions. Never entrust a candidate's first impression of your company to a boor.

Check on the headhunter's track record in the IT sector and find out how many positions he or she has filled that are similar to yours. How long did it take to fill those slots? (More than three months is too long.) How many searches were aborted? (Twenty-five percent are never completed, but the invoice is due anyway.)

What's the retention rate for those candidates? How does the recruiter familiarize himself with the client's culture, industry, personnel needs and inner workings? (You need somebody with a tried-and-true method and the confidence to insist that it is followed.)

Ethical recruiters honor a two-year off-limits rule when they accept an assignment. They won't approach your people during that time, and they won't attempt to fill openings for you from another client's ranks. Find out which companies are off-limits to the recruiter you're considering. If you're convinced the talent you need is behind one of those doors, choose another firm. But don't be too hasty: the best headhunters are plugged into networks you don't know exist.

The best headhunter in the world can't succeed without *access* and *information*. This means access to people throughout your organization—up to and including top management—and in-depth information about your business plan, your staffing plan and your hiring successes and failures.

Keep in mind that your recruiter does more than drum up candidates. He or she is also responsible for *selling* the opportunity, and top people often have five or six competing offers. Your recruiter needs every possible advantage. (Case in point: the Connecticut company whose managers didn't think to mention the free on-site daycare during interviews.)

Briefing the recruiter will take a day or more, and yes, it will undoubtedly irritate you to spend that much time bringing this person up to speed. *If he's as good as he says he is, why can't he figure this stuff out on his own? I **gave** him a job description and an org chart!* Blowing off the front-end briefing is a huge mistake, and the best recruiters won't let you do it. "Investing time and energy on the front end makes it much less painful on the back end," says Atlanta-based contract recruiter Dottie Regan. "You can't learn the company's culture and hiring situation in a one-hour meeting."

Common misconceptions about headhunters can spoil a potentially good working relationship. Knowing what to expect will make you a better client. A few tips:

*Don't assume the recruiter has met the candidates he or she sends you.* As we mentioned earlier, contingency and e-cruiting are volume businesses. Leisurely lunches and face-to-face interviews are time-consuming, therefore rare. Unless you've contracted with a retained search consultant, there's no guarantee that recruiter and candidates have actually met in person.

*Don't assume the recruiter will conduct background or reference checks.* Except for retained search firms, few do this automatically. Some won't do it at all; others do it only for an additional fee. If you want it done or need credentials and work history confirmed, expect to negotiate for these services.

*Don't assume a recruiter won't bite the hand that feeds.* Find out what the recruiter's anti-raid policies are. Some will actually solicit your employees on one line while calling you for business on the other. Diligent reference checking will help weed out these vipers. Working with industry-certified professionals helps, too: the good ones take their association's code of ethics seriously.

*Don't think you can treat recruiters shabbily and get away with it.* They have constant contact with people you want on your payroll, and their influence is undeniable. Trash a recruiter and you can be buried every day and never know it.

*Don't blame the recruiter for bad hires.* The quality of your staffing plan and ideal hire profile, the quality of your up-front briefing, and the inside access you give your headhunters determine 85 percent of the results they deliver. Garbage in, garbage out.

*Don't assume that big firms are always better.* It's often exactly the opposite. "The smaller, privately-owned boutiques are usually most successful at recruiting, but they're also the worst marketers," says Alan Lee of Careerelite.com. "You usually have to find them through word of mouth."

Is there a company on the planet that doesn't claim, "Our people are our most important asset?" To see if that's true, check out the human resource department's rank in the corporate pecking order.

If the head of HR doesn't report to the CEO, and the public relations budget's a lot bigger than the recruiting budget, the department is out of the mainstream and will never be fully effective. "There's an easy way to find out how top management perceives human resources," says Lee. "Just take a look at how many people in the company want to cross-pollinate their career with an assignment in HR."

Marginalizing your recruiters is like sending a fighter into the ring with a bag over his head. "The leader of the HR organization *must* have a seat at the management table," says Kevin Shigley, sourcing strategist for iXL Enterprises. "It's hard to drive change from the bottom up."

Turning in-house staff into a recruiting powerhouse calls for corporate-wide commitment (witness Cisco Systems, Trilogy Software and eBay), and you've got to start somewhere. Here are the fundamentals.

*Train your recruiting staff on the technology tools they need to do the job.* "When I started here, there were 20,000 resumés in the applicant tracking system that nobody knew what to do with," says one technology company recruiter. "The recruiters hadn't been given any hands-on system training. The resumés just sat there gathering dust."

Do your people know how to conduct basic Internet searches? Do they all record applicant contact information the same way? Have you standardized your interview techniques and processes across departments, cities, regions? If not, you're paying a 25 percent to 50 percent premium for redundancy and errors.

*Make sure your recruiters know how your company makes money.* Have they actually seen the product being manufactured, the software being tested, the service being delivered, and the customer being supported? Do they understand business basics and communicate clearly with line managers? (Would they even recognize your line managers if they saw them?)

An astonishing number of executives can't answer "yes" to any of these questions—if they can answer them at all.

*Expect accountability.* That old maxim, "HR's a soft discipline—you can't really measure it," is baloney. Figure out what you need to quantify, then set performance standards. Internal client satisfaction levels, retention rates, applicant quality, the number of calls made, the number of people hired ... choose any and all metrics that matter to your organization.

We've said it before and we'll say it again: the right recruiter can be worth millions to your company. Whether on staff or outside, certain traits set the headhunting crème de la crème apart from B players.

*They've developed a deep, rich personal network.* The top 2 percent of recruiters in a community influence 95 percent of the CEO and board level placements in that community.

*They are utterly discreet.* Sensitive information is safe with them, even after the search is complete.

*They have an innate ability to separate fluff from substance.* Good headhunters probe for results, patterns, and character, not showmanship. They know how to separate tap dancers from the real thing.

*They are skilled at sleuthing, assessing, selling, and presenting.* The best recruiters are cultural anthropologists: intent listeners who don't miss much when it comes to human behavior. They're also articulate, persuasive and opinionated.

*They're passionate about making a difference.* By definition, recruiters have an enormous influence over the lives of the people and companies they touch. The best headhunters understand and accept this responsibility.

"Boiling it down, two things are important in this business," says Jim Hogg, president of Pennsylvania-based Whittlesea & Associates.

"First, you need to understand a person's passion. Second, you need to understand a person's talent. Put the two together and there's the chance to create a pretty explosive situation—one that can make a positive impact on any enterprise."

# Your Web Site: First Stop for Prospective Employees

Half of the companies with recruiting components on their Web sites are doing nothing but the basics. They post job information and openings, but candidates submit applications through traditional channels like email and fax. More sophisticated employers are pushing the technology as far as it will go with online application processing, prescreening and testing, but they're still in the minority.

There's no question, though, that the entire corporate recruiting process is well on the way to becoming an online supply chain. iLogos Research in San Francisco went out on a limb recently with a prediction that every company in the Global 500 will be a fully e-centric recruiter by 2003. That's a pretty strong statement given the chaotic state of current technology, but the message is clear. If your company isn't on the bandwagon, you'd better move fast.

One of the most aggressive online employers is Cisco Systems, which hires 8,000 people a year and receives 81 percent of its resumés over the Internet. Cisco's machine is so fine-tuned the company has shaved 68 days off the hiring cycle and slashed its per-hire cost to $6,500. (The industry average is around $11,000.)

Cisco has mastered the concept of creating an online community where browsers come back again and again. The company's recruiting prowess is so well publicized there's no point in rehashing the details here, but if you go to *www.cisco.com* you can see for yourself what's possible when branding and recruiting fuse on a corporate Web site.

### What does a good Web site look like?

Good recruiting sites aren't necessarily glamorous or glitzy. They're a magnet for job hunters, curiosity seekers ("I'm not in the market, but if the right thing came along..."), competitors and recruiters datamining for information, so they have to be easy for desirables to use without giving away the store to everybody else. Don't even think about looks, however, until the site's architecture and navigation are as streamlined and intuitive as they can possibly be.

- Make sure contact information is never more than a click away. Include a contact name (fictional is OK), your company's name, full address, phone and fax numbers and email address. (Use a free email service. Corporate addresses are a dead giveaway to your email structure, and clever recruiters have a field day with them.) Don't forget driving directions and a map to your location. When a candidate's running out the door for an interview but can't remember your street number, the last thing she wants to do is slog through a corporate mission statement to figure out where you are.
- Graphics are good until they're overdone. Anything that takes more than five or six seconds to download is irritating and finally drives viewers away. Don't fall in love with special effects. Edit first-draft copy by half, then read it again to see what more you can eliminate. We read computer screens only about half as fast as we read ink on paper, so don't be verbose. Bullet points work best.
- Links are a great way to to enhance and expand the impact of your site. When describing your company's stock option plan, link to sites that calculate the likely value of a potential

investment. When you showcase your firm's renovated ware-house offices, link to the "most livable city" award your town received last year. Connect the paragraph about your com-pany's tuition reimbursement program to local universities.

- In the so-obvious-it-doesn't-bear-repeating category: spell out acronyms and proofread everything before it's posted. Typos are rampant on even the prissiest Web sites.
- Hire a professional to create and maintain your site, and pay the going rate. If developing Web sites is what you do for a living, you'll probably have to bring in an outside contractor or it won't get done at all.
- You'll be sick of the design in less than a year, but *don't* change the overall look and feel unless the following sit-uations apply:
  - o Your company has launched a new corporate-wide mar-keting campaign
  - o Your firm has changed its name, been acquired, or under-gone similar identity issues
  - o Your site was originally designed by a well-meaning ama-teur, but now you have the resources to do it right

### Content begins and ends with WIIFM

The only thing a visitor to your Web site cares about is WIIFM: *What's in it for me?*

It's laughable how many companies completely ignore this principle.

"Are you selling jobs? No!," says Eric Jaquith, our Atlanta-based contract recruiter. You're selling the company and the idea of working there. Show me a snapshot of a day in the life of Joe Programmer. Invite me to correspond online with somebody. Ask if I want to be on the email newsletter list. Give me as many rea-sons as you can to stay in touch."

Jaquith is one of those people who are adamant about keeping job descriptions out of public view and pacing applicants through a subtle online qualification process.

"This is an information exchange," he says. "You tell me some-thing, I tell you something. I don't want people surfing my open-ings and disappearing."

There are countless ways to make your site more interactive and reflect your company's culture, style and values. Create an FAQ page that answers all the questions that pop up in the hiring process. (How often do we get paid? Do you have direct deposit? How close is public transportation? What's the dress code? Can I bring my dog to work?)

Highlight verbatim quotes from employees (no last names) telling why they chose your company. List ten reasons why people come to Bigbucks when they could work anywhere they want. Create a chat room and an email newsletter. Anything goes as long as common sense prevails: don't spotlight individual employees, publish company directories or show captioned photos of the departmental beach party. You don't want to give headhunters any more information than necessary.

Customized online information packets are another way to open a dialogue with applicants. With a $39 software package called Catch The Web, you can capture relevant pages from your site and email them to the candidate with a note along these lines: "Yes, we have openings, and here's a custom snapshot of what might interest you here at Bigbucks."

If your site is big and unwieldy, this is an easy way to make sure visitors see what interests them and skip the rest. If you prepare the packets by department, geographic location, functional area, or any other breakdown that makes sense for your firm, they're easy to send on demand.

### Politics and the Webmaster

Who's got responsibility for your Web site? Who's got authority? If they're not one and the same, odds are good your site is caught in a corporate quagmire.

If your Webmaster reports to IT, but the HR people have final copy approval and the marketing department writes the content, watch out.

The scenario goes something like this. The writer produces some lively copy, which the HR people redline until it doesn't say much of anything. It then goes to the IT department, where it sits for a week due to a programmer backlog. When it's finally posted there's a typo in it.

If you're a hapless manager on the sidelines, this is pretty discouraging. You'll have to figure out where the real control is or find a way to work around the system. There's no easy answer, and unless branding and recruiting initiatives come straight from your CEO, you'll have to resign yourself to a site that doesn't serve potential employees as well as it could.

If it's any consolation, one of the most successful companies in the world didn't even *have* a recruiting Web site until 1999. "Believe it or not, a big part of the problem was that nobody could agree on what it should say," admits a former Coca-Cola employee.

See all those job listings on your Web site? They make a poacher's eyes light right up. About the only way to make your company more vulnerable is to install a dial-by-name directory on your voice mail system. Detailed job descriptions and email addresses don't belong on your Web site.

Admittedly, this is a contrarian point of view. If you don't use your recruiting pages to post jobs, what *are* you going to do with them?

Use them to spark an ongoing dialogue between your company and potential employees.

When your site is nothing but a clearing house, you miss a huge opportunity to reach people not yet in the job market. Building online relationships with candidates long before you need them is the secret to managing the IT talent shortage.

Visitors who enter as job hunters may ultimately turn into customers or stockholders, and vice versa. A site packed with useful content is one of the most powerful branding tools in your company's marketing arsenal. (And if you couldn't care less about marketing, think of it as a practical way to build a talent pipeline.)

**PART
II**

# Choosing the Right Candidate: Finding "Keepers"

# How *Not* to Hire Technical Talent

You've heard the statistic: the cost of a bad hire is anywhere from 2 to 6 times the employee's annual salary, not counting any customer relationships or deals damaged along the way.

*Sure*, you say. *But if I knew up front that it was a bad hire, I wouldn't have done it, would I?*

Maybe and maybe not. Some organizational psychologists claim we make a go/no-go assessment about a job applicant within the first 30 seconds and spend the rest of the interview gathering evidence to reinforce that decision. This may be an exaggeration but there's no question that subjectivity and down-right desperation are behind plenty of job offers.

Managers charged with hiring technical talent find that certain mistakes crop up over and over. Here's a rundown on those that seem to take the biggest toll. There are others, of course, but avoiding these will go a long way toward keeping you out of trouble.

**Never hire:**
- *Without a clear plan*
- *In your own image*
- *Because they worked for Microsoft (or your biggest competitor)*

- *Because they were screened by non-IT staff*
- *Simply because they were referred by a headhunter*
- *Based solely on a reputation and a resumé*
- *Because it was the best you could do at the time*

### Hiring without a clear plan

You're saying to yourself, *"Plan? You've got to be kidding. Who's got time to plan?* Nobody does. You've got to make the time.

We're not talking about a five-pound treatise (although a comprehensive plan is ideal). And we're not talking about job descriptions. The staffing plan template on page 119 can be adapted as you see fit.

If you're really plan-averse, your staffing plan can be as simple as a three-column list on a single sheet of paper. The whole idea is to clarify the skills and aptitudes you *have* on staff, identify the ones you'd *like* to have, and figure out where the gaps are. Getting this down in writing forces you to think through your situation clearly and see the whole picture. Without this, you'll make the same hiring mistakes over and over.

A staffing plan lets you focus your energy on looking in the *right* places for the *right* people and asking the *right* questions when you're face to face with candidates. It's certainly tempting to take the course of least resistance and simply look for warm bodies, but matching a candidate's abilities and ambitions against the work at hand and your company's culture is critical. Done well, this step can literally double your employee retention rate.

### Hiring in your own image

There's a name for this. It's called the halo effect. You've been successful, after all; if you could just clone yourself, this thing would work.

It seldom turns out that way. No matter how many qualities you share with a candidate, this person is not you. He or she is *guaranteed* to respond differently, make decisions differently, and perform differently than you would in exactly the same situations.

Even when those decisions are entirely appropriate, you'll be disappointed because you unconsciously expected a different approach.

The more similarities there seem to be between you and a candidate, the more vulnerable you are to the halo effect. Let's say you're interviewing someone who, it turns out, went to the same college you did. He or she has like interests, knows a lot of the same people you do, even shares your sense of humor. You establish an almost instant rapport, and you feel this is someone you can depend upon to get the job done. This person's resumé experience looks great, too. No-brainer!

Or is it? Odds are good that you won't probe as carefully, or as deeply, with this candidate as you would with someone else, simply because you (quite naturally) made a series of rapid assumptions. Great rapport is so compelling that it short-circuits the hiring process. Prevent this by establishing a multiple-interviewer process and giving a fair hearing to every interviewer's opinions.

It's been proven over and over that diversity wins in the long run, whether it relates to age, race, gender, cultural origin, or experience. Stick to your ideal hire profile and enlist an interview committee to prevent hiring a whole team of "mini me's."

### Hiring because they worked for Microsoft (or your biggest competitor)

Now that you know about the halo effect, let's talk about bio bias. There are certain technology companies whose names on a resumé impart instant credibility. Microsoft is one of them (although this seems to be true the further you get, geographically, from Seattle.) As an employer, you're vulnerable to bio bias the instant you read a resumé from a candidate with ultra-blue-chip experience. The danger's particularly high when this candidate has spent two or more years each with a series of brand-name employers.

It's tempting to bring this person in immediately for an interview. That's fine, if on paper the worker's qualifications fit your staffing plan and ideal hire profile. But if there's no fit (the programmer's expertise is Java and he or she has no management experience; you're an AS/400 shop and you need a seasoned project leader) or a forced fit, think twice before you commit valuable interview time. The idea of bringing in a crème de la crème alum, even if that background is the candidate's *only* qualification, is almost irresistible. The beauty of a staffing plan is that it protects you from buying on impulse.

Beware of bio bias, too, when hiring people who have worked for your competitor. In 1987 Digital Equipment Company decided to go after IBM customers. DEC aggressively recruited employees with Big Blue experience, hiring many people who'd opted for "early retirement" from IBM. Some worked out well. But others actually retired a second time—while still on DEC's payroll.

Experience with a competitor does not automatically translate into success with your company. Candidates must have the skills to do the work at hand—and they *must* be compatible with your corporate culture, which is probably very different from their last employer's.

### Hiring because they were screened by non-IT staff

Managers lament the fact that well-intentioned human resource people often screen out good candidates simply because they don't know what to look for. The HR people, on the other hand, are frustrated because hiring managers don't make their selection criteria crystal-clear.

This communication gap is a serious problem. In many organizations, HR people don't have the technical expertise to screen IT candidates beyond documented experience with programming languages. The intention is good; the results are not.

If you work in an organization where the human resource department is charged with screening, you need to provide the HR people with written job profiles and *prioritized* ideal hire criteria for each position. If you need a C++ programmer with critical thinking skills and supervisory experience, make it clear to the HR people which skills you absolutely can't live without (even though you need everything on the list). Selecting for too many things is counterproductive. Every criterion you add to the list reduces the pool of eligible candidates.

Some things, such as certain technical skills, can be taught within a reasonable time frame; others can't. As Bridget O'Connor, senior vice president of IT at Lehman Brothers, puts it, "Give me the person with the right balance of common sense and logic and I can teach them technology. Technology is not an occult art. The real issue is 'can they apply it?'" Technology will have changed ninety days after your new employee is in the door. Passion for technology is much more important than knowledge of a single language.

### Hiring simply because they were referred by a headhunter

Never assume that any and all candidates referred by a head-hunter are qualified for the position. Unless the recruiter is conducting a retained search (being paid in advance) the name of the game is volume. Many recruiters never meet the people they forward to you. You must still screen and evaluate each candidate.

Recruiters and search firms are as vulnerable to bio bias as anyone else. For a recruiter looking for someone with SAP skills, a resumé from a member of the SAP implementation team at Company X will rise right to the top of the pile. If you don't charge that recruiter with checking out the story behind the implementation (Was it successful? What role did the candidate play in its success?), expect to do the background work yourself. Keep in mind that recruiters who work on contingency—that is, they're paid only when they place an applicant—are not really interested in finding evidence that their candidate *isn't* a fit. This doesn't mean they're unethical; it simply means they're probably not as objective as you might assume.

### Hiring based solely upon a reputation and a resumé

This is a subtle variation on the bio bias theme. Technology communities—no matter how big or how small—are pretty tightly knit. Sooner or later everybody knows (or has heard of) just about everybody else. Third-party endorsement is incredibly convincing, so it's easy to waive due diligence when you're considering candidates whose reputations precede them.

When we asked an executive who headed up the IT area for a major software company to describe his biggest hiring mistake, he told us about a situation early in his career. "We'd just finished a huge NT conversion, and when I hired a guy to lead the group chartered with supporting it, I bought his reputation without doing an in-depth analysis.

"His tendency when confronted with a problem was to fall back on what he knew. At one point he actually recommended scrapping the NT installation and replacing it with UNIX, which he considered a technically 'pure' solution. No fiscal perspective at all. He didn't have pragmatism . . . and I didn't interview for it."

When the last CEO of the former Digital Equipment Corporation stepped into his position, he staffed several top slots with people who had big reputations. Each came from different companies with different cultures; each was used to being the boss. Digital, however, operated by consensus and matrix management. (Employees used to joke that "99 to one is a tie.")

The result? "The Battle of the Titans." Within 18 months, all three of the new senior people were gone and a number of home-grown executives left to run other firms. The company never recovered from the brain drain.

### Hiring because it was the best you could do at the time

This is the "to hell with it—we can't afford to be choosy" syndrome. You're running a department with a backlog of open jobs, an overworked staff and tasks piling up by the day. The pressure to hire—to hire *anyone*—is enormous. But if the candidate you're considering doesn't meet your specifications, don't do it. "Availability" is not a valid job qualification.

The consequences of a poor hiring decision are so predictable they can actually be charted. Figure 8.1 depicts the vicious circle created by making one bad hire. It starts when you bring on someone who lacks the skills to do a particular job. For whatever reason, the person can't produce the quantity or quality of

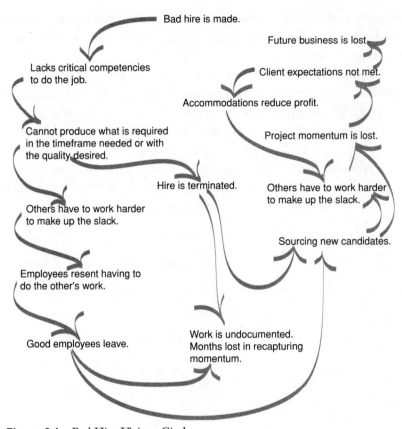

**Figure 8.1**   Bad Hire Vicious Circle

work you need in a timely fashion. Others in the work group have to make up the slack. Resentment sets in (whether the manager realizes it or not) and morale drops. Some employees—often the most talented—resign. Eventually the poor-performing employee leaves too.

All these employees have left chunks of their work undocumented, so the process to recapture what was done gets underway. This can take months and cannot be legitimately billed to the client (whether internal or external). Now you have more than one position to fill, and depending upon the skills you need and how well you planned for turnover, this will take about 90 days.

Meanwhile, back at the ranch, other team members are working harder to make up for the vacant slots. Project deadlines are slipping and the client is beginning to complain. You make accommodations to appease the client, and the pressure on margins and deadlines increases.

At this point the executive team is usually pulled in to solve the problem. The project team continues to struggle, the client relationship grows more strained, and the executive group is now focused on emergency repairs instead of growing the company.

Photocopy this page and put it somewhere handy. Next time you interview a candidate who's ready and willing but doesn't fit your ideal hire profile, take another look at the vicious circle and ask yourself, "Is this *really* a good idea?"

# How to Use Your Company's Culture to Compete for Talent

**What does culture have to do with hiring, anyway?**

The culture of a company is a shared mindset about the way business is conducted, problems are approached, and employees are treated. "The culture" is the most frequently cited reason for joining a company and staying with a company, and when a hire doesn't work out, cultural mis-fit is one of the most frequently cited reasons. It's important to understand your culture and the type of person who is going to thrive in it *before* you hire.

Whenever I speak with a client I ask them to describe their culture. Often there's a pause, and then they say something like, "Well, we do whatever it takes to get the job done." That's a red flag to me that the culture of the company—one of its most important strategic advantages—is an accident. Whatever your culture is, it can be strategically shaped. This chapter explores the strategic implications of your company's culture, and explains how you can turn it into an asset to be used to compete for tech talent.

The culture of successful companies ties to their reason for being, and the principles that inform it probably evolved out of the vision that started the company. The energy and sense of purpose that guides your actions comes from the vision of what you wanted to accomplish. Perhaps others, energized by your vision, joined in the endeavor. And before long, you had a sizeable group working on the task. As the size of the group became larger, the sense of purpose became less clear. As new people join the group they bring their "stuff", which is different from the "stuff" of the founders. What was once clear becomes, well, muddy. This is why you hear CEOs like Carly Fiorino of Hewlett-Packard talk about returning to the garage where the company was founded. What she is seeking is a return to the energy and vibrancy of the startup called H-P.

Our research tells us that there is no one successful culture. There are many. The important thing is clarity about that vision and purposefulness in adhering to it.

Gabe was a high flyer at an Internet startup. He led the company from ground zero through IPO, took the money and left. A conservative bank in the Midwest was looking to establish a web presence and hired Gabe. He lasted ninety days. Why? He did not fit the culture.

Eileen, a software designer at Application Partners, joined the company because it supports the idea that its people should have a life. She's been offered a job with Whiz Technology. At WT people work long hours, but make great money. It is not at all unusual to find people working all weekend to get a job done. How likely are they to recruit Eileen away? And if they do, will she stay? Not likely.

### How can you tell what your culture is

There is no single "right" culture for all companies. But there is a culture that is right—or wrong—for a given company and a given individual. Cameron & Quinn (1999) described culture from a perspective of competing values. As a company sets its priorities and develops its strategy, it will most likely favor one value more than another. No company is absolutely one thing or another. Our experience suggests, however, that if a company ranks itself as equally high in two opposing factors, it is probably struggling with its identity. Nevertheless, the position a company takes on each of these values shapes its culture.

**Lifestyle Focus vs. Results Focus:** The Lifestyle culture tends to be family oriented and relationship based. What matters is the quality of life of the employees. Generally speaking, lifestyle companies develop a culture that focuses on work/life balance. Employees that gravitate toward lifestyle companies are willing to sacrifice financial perquisites in order to have the balance they seek.

The Results culture may care about its employees, but sees them as drivers of profit. The firm looks at the impact of its employees on the bottom line, and seeks to maximize productivity. This culture drives people hard toward achievement, and employees are willing to sacrifice personal time in favor of financial rewards. Lehman Brothers is an example of a results culture. Although it values individual lifestyle choices, those who are rewarded financially and with other indicators of success are the employees who are willing to go the "extra mile."

**Technology Focus vs. Market Focus:** The technology-focused culture competes in the marketplace based on having the latest technology. These companies tend to look inward, tapping the creativity of their personnel to develop the technically pure solution.

The market-focused culture is concerned primarily with conforming its technology to meet market demand. They will settle for a B-minus product and complement it with a superior go-to-market strategy. They may aggressively target competitors.

**Process Focus vs. Innovation Focus:** Process cultures tend to be more formal and structured. Often mature, they use structure to bring an element of discipline and consistency to their work. Compaq's Professional Services Group is a process-driven group. Working on very large projects where multiple people will develop parts of a customer solution, methodology is the critical glue in holding the project to high consistency and quality standards. Andersen Consulting is another example of a company where the focus on process allows consultants with little business experience to team effectively with senior, more experienced consultants to deliver the product. The process is the glue that makes it work.

Innovation cultures are energized by discovery, vision and creativity. They tend to be less formal, and probably find process too confining. A company that builds computer animation for video and Internet products might be an innovation culture. Dot coms—basically built on an idea—may be innovation cultures. The ability to reconceptualize itself as the market moves allows the firm to survive. In innovation cultures, the idea rules.

Selecting prospective employees for culture fit requires understanding both your corporate culture and the type of person who will be happy in that environment.

Here's a quick way to understand your company's culture. It will take about an hour to do as a business team and will provide great insights.

1. Gather as a group and have each participant, working alone, answer the questions in Table 9.1 by distributing 50 points to the opposing statements in each row. Instruct participants to give more points to statements that are more like your culture, and fewer points to statements that are less like it.

2. While participants are completing their individual evaluations, write each of the two opposing statements on a flip chart and post them on the wall. There are two sets of opposing statements for each set of opposing values. Cluster the statements according to the culture values.

3. Have each team member come to the wall and "distribute" their 50 points among each of the opposing statements by writing their number next to the statement on the flip chart.

4. Total up the number for each statement.

5. Total up the number for each opposing value and input each number into the Datasheet of the Culture Profile (Table 9.1).

The table will automatically generate your profile on the downloadable graph provided in Figure 9.1. The opposing values that have the highest percentages represent the dominant values in

**Table 9.1**  Culture Diagnostic Survey

| No. | Statement | Points | Statement | Points |
|---|---|---|---|---|
| | **Lifestyle** | | **Results** | |
| 1 | People in our company value work/life balance. We get the job done, and then we go home. | | People in our company value results. We expect our people will make personal sacrifices to get the job done. | |
| 2 | We place a higher value on the quality of life of our employees than we do on results. | | Our primary consideration in making commitments is the impact of the decision on the bottom line. | |
| | **Total Lifestyle** | | **Total Results** | |
| | **Technology** | | **Market** | |
| 3 | People in our company pride themselves on producing technology of extraordinary quality. | | People in our company are focused on the customer and on what's going on in the marketplace. | |
| 4 | People in our company like to be working with leading-edge solutions. | | People in our company will aggressively compete for business, and we usually win. | |
| | **Total Technology** | | **Total Market** | |
| | **Process** | | **Innovation** | |
| 5 | People in our company believe that using process and methodology to design our products make for stability, repeatability, and consistency. | | People in our company are energized by ideas and vision. | |
| 6 | We look for repeatability in our solutions, and tend to discourage customization. | | We see the uniqueness in each situation, and provide custom solutions to our customers. | |
| | **Total Process** | | **Total Innovation** | |

SOURCE: Copyright McGraw-Hill 2001. To customize this handout for your audience, download it from (*www.books.mcgraw-hill.com/training/download http://www.books.mcgraw-hill.com/training/download*). The document can then be opened, edited, and printed using Microsoft Word or other popular word-processing software.

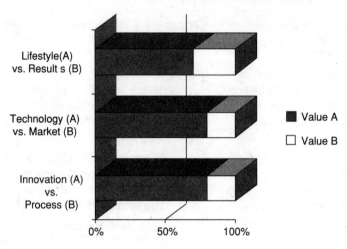

**Figure 9.1**   Culture Profile

your culture. The closer your culture is to the middle of a dimension in the opposing value chart, the more your company will possess attributes of both aspects of the opposing values.

Once you have plotted your culture, you can then prioritize those aspects of your culture that suggest favoring certain capabilities. Figure 9.1 is an example of a culture that is strongly motivated by innovation and technology. It values lifestyle slightly more than results, and would probably emphasize the importance of receiving goals as well.

### Culture as strategy

Understanding—and clarifying—your company's culture makes sense because it affects:

- The type of people who will be attracted to your company
- How you motivate employees, and galvanize them to action
- How you retain employees, and immunize yourself from competitive recruiting practices
- How you compensate employees to both attract and retain them

Following are descriptions of the different culture profiles, taking into account some of their strategic implications.

*Lifestyle Cultures:* Since lifestyle cultures take actions and make decisions based on providing a high quality of life and balance between the demands of the marketplace and the employee's personal life, employees who *"want a life"* will be attracted to a lifestyle company. They will be willing to make financial sacrifices to work there. The attraction of the Lifestyle culture will offset higher salaries and other compensation perquisites offered by competing cultures. If yours is a lifestyle culture you may offer daycare for children, assistance in finding eldercare for an aging parent, and paid leave for major events in employees' lives.

*Results Cultures:* Since results cultures take actions and make decisions based on providing good return on investment to shareholders, employees who *"want big bucks"* will be attracted to a results company. Motivate them with feedback on individual accomplishment. The results culture must significantly compensate employees to offset competing offers by other companies with financial and other perqs to top performers.

*Innovation Cultures:* People who thrive on doing new things will enjoy working in the Innovation Culture. Employees who *"want to go where no man has gone before"* will enjoy working here. They will be willing to make financial sacrifices to do work they enjoy. Look for people who have many creative outlets—technology and music, art, etc. Stress the creative side of your company to attract them.

*Technology Cultures:* People who enjoy honing their technology skills place high value on working in a technology culture. Employees who *"want to learn hot technology"* will enjoy working here. Techies that fit this profile see the technical reputation of the company as an additional attractor. Consider creating a sandbox where employees can collaborate on developing new frontiers. Look for candidates in special interest groups.

*Market Cultures:* People who thrive on customer satisfaction particularly enjoy working in a market culture. They are generally motivated to achieve, are good communicators, and *"like people"*.

*Process Cultures*: Process focus adds an element of discipline to the art of creating technology. It also provides a method for introducing junior resources into an ongoing project team. People who *"like discipline and structure"* appreciate the balance and consistency that process brings to technology. People who like to create one-off technical solutions will be very frustrated in this environment.

### Managing within a specific culture

Working in each culture will feel different. Managing in each culture will bring a different set of challenges.

The *Innovation/Technology* culture is abuzz with discovery. Employees will be energized talking about the latest new product or solution they have developed. The management challenge will be to focus the creative juices on producing the products and solutions that will have the greatest impact.

The *Market/Innovation* culture is concerned about providing the best product to meet a customer's requirements. Management's challenge will be to focus innovation where needed, and draw on experience where it is relevant.

The *Technology/Process* culture is all about meeting milestones, keeping commitments, managing scope, and delivering excellence. Often a systems integration or technical consulting firm or the application development arm of an IT shop, this group is all about applying new technology to solve customer problems. Management's challenge is to continue to apply methodology to the process of innovation, and to drive replicability in methods, models, and solutions.

The *Market/Process* culture applies structure and methodology to solve customer problems. Their go-to-market strategy will focus on providing customer-demanded functionality as quickly and economically as possible. This culture would be interested in mass customization—development of a core technology base that provided opportunities to minimally and economically configure the technology to meet some limited customer preferences.

Table 9.2 provides a matrix that suggests the most likely individual capabilities to support a particular culture. Compensation to attract and retain employees based on your culture is indicated in the chart as well. Generally speaking, you will have to compensate employees more based on the level of sacrifice they are making.

**Table 9.2** Compete for Talent Based on Your Company's Culture

| Culture focus | How employees describe it ... | Look for people who demonstrate ... | Compensation strategy* |
|---|---|---|---|
| Lifestyle | "I'm very important to to this company. They do everything possible to make this a fun place to work." | **Collaboration:** Esprit de corps is very important in a lifestyle culture. Select people who work well in teams. | • Medium |
| Results | "This company rewards hard work. The harder I work the more I'm rewarded." | **Performance:** Achievement motivation and a record of having consistently met or exceeded goals. | • High |
| Technology | "Our products (solutions) are leading edge. I get to work on the latest and greatest here." | **Technical Acumen:** Select people who are proficient in the technology you need, and look for a zeal to learn new things. | • Medium to High based on skill level. • High for superstars. |
| Market | "I know that what I do is directly related to what customers want and need. That means a lot to me." | **Relating Skills:** Select people who can interact with customers, can communicate effectively with them, and influence their thinking. | • High |
| Process | "We build quality solutions step-by-step. I learned how to solve problems methodically here." | **Sense of Urgency:** Select people who can organize a task to get the job done on time, on budget, and on spec. | • High |
| Innovation | "I really enjoy building something new, and that's what we do here." | **Active Learning:** Select people who have a passion for learning new things. | • Medium |

*Compensation should be considered relative to range of salaries and other compensation benefits in your geography.

If you have a results emphasis in your culture, you will be asking potential employees to give up some personal time and freedom. If the results culture also places a percentage of the employee's income at risk based on performance, the element of risk will also have to be factored into the equation. If, on top of that, you are also asking employees to grind out repeatable code to the same customer over an extended period of time, you are asking that they also sacrifice personal growth. You get the idea.

### How to find someone who will fit in your culture

Having plotted your culture, you can now refer to the chart in Table 9.2[1] and understand how employees view your culture and who will be attracted to your company. When we get to Chapter 11, we will be discussing how to build an Ideal Hire Profile. The capabilities that support your culture would be included in any Ideal Hire Profile you are building for an individual position.

In Chapter 14, we cover how to interview for culture compatibility. Our research clearly shows that people stay with—or leave—a company because of the culture.

### Conclusion

If your company operates on sheer adrenaline, the world's best programmer is a high-risk hire if he or she is uncomfortable with quick decisions and tight deadlines. If your environment's quiet and focused, a gregarious project manager who needs lots of social interaction will drive coworkers nuts (and vice versa). It's important to see your corporate landscape (i.e. culture and style) clearly so you can hire based upon who will complement the picture.

Be aware, however, that choosing candidates best suited to your corporate culture is *not* the same as creating an organization full of lookalikes. As we mentioned in Chapter 8, diversity is important. Every group needs a cross-section of personalities, experience and skills to do great work.

---

[1]Copyright McGraw-Hill 2001. To customize this handout for your audience, download it from (*www.books.mcgraw-hill.com/training/download http://www.books.mcgraw-hill.com/training/download*). The document can then be opened, edited, and printed using Microsoft Word or other popular word-processing software.

# 10

# How to Create a Staffing Plan

### What is a staffing plan?

A staffing plan is an orderly way of deciding how you are going to organize your workgroup and what resources you'll need to get the job done. It gives you in one snapshot a picture of what talent you have, what personnel movement you anticipate, and the kinds of openings you both have and anticipate. Taking time to do an annual staffing plan, and updating it quarterly to reflect changes in your organization will save time, wasted effort, and costly mis-hires.

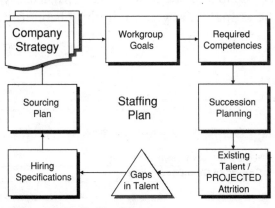

**Figure 10.1**   Staffing Plan

## The Steps in Creating a Staffing Plan

1. Understand the goals of your corporate strategy.
2. Describe your workgroup's goals and the structure you will need to achieve them.
3. Evaluate your current talent.
4. Plan for succession.
5. Anticipate attrition.
6. Define hiring specifications
7. Develop sourcing strategy.

*Step 1: Understand the goals of your corporate strategy.* Before you can decide how to get there, you need to know where you're going. The corporate strategy is the big picture—why your company exists, who your customer is, and what you intend to offer that customer. Your marching orders come as a result of the strategy. The staffing plan is your road map of how you are going to get there.

Do you expect to enter new markets, introduce products, or offload lines of business within the next year or so? Each of these potential moves would affect your human resources needs. Are you preparing to acquire another company, or to be acquired? If so, you will be trying to integrate additional people into your department, or somebody will be attempting to integrate your department into theirs. Seeking funding? Planning an IPO? Where does your company want you to be in two years? Skills that are essential to one strategy aren't particularly useful to another, so be as specific as you can in this phase of the staffing plan analysis.

---

**Staffing Plan**
*Step 1: Understand the goals of your corporate strategy.*

ACTION: Identify the main goals of your corporate strategy:

| | Corporate Goal Description |
|---|---|
| | |
| | |

**Figure 10.2** Step 1 Input

In Step 1 look at your corporate strategy and identify the specific goals that the company will have to achieve. These goals form the basis for evaluating your staffing needs.

*Step 2: Describe your work group's goals and the organizational structure you will need to achieve them.* If your strategy is the description of where you need to go, your structure is the vehicle that is designed to get you there. Just as you wouldn't want to drive a Jaguar nowhere but the grocery store, you want to use the most efficient organizational structure to achieve your goals. Your goal in Step 2 is to identify your workgroup goals and identify and remove any structural hindrances to achieving them. To do this ask yourself two questions: "What must I accomplish this year in order to succeed? and "What is the most efficient way I can organize to get the job done?"

Let's say that you're an offensive coach on a football team, and your team's strategy is to increase the number of points your team makes by passing the ball. Today, you have a strong ground game,

---

**Staffing Plan**
*Step 2: Describe your workgroup's goals and the structure you will need to achieve them.*

ACTIONS:
(A) List the goals of your workgroup in the column entitled "Workgroup Goal Description".
(B) List your plan to achieve each goal in the column entitled "Plan to Achieve".
(C) Insert or attach a copy of the proposed organization chart that you will use to achieve your goals.
(D) List the roles (Example: Project Manager) you will need in the column entitled "Identified Workgroup Roles", and identify whether you (1) already have them, (2) plan to grow (train & develop) them (3) outsource the work or (3) buy (hire externally) them in the appropriate columns.

| A. Workgroup Goal Description | B. Plan to Achieve |
|---|---|
| | |
| | |
| | |

**C. Organization:**
(Insert organization chart here.)

| D. Identified Workgroup Roles | Have | Grow | Outsource | Buy (Hire) |
|---|---|---|---|---|
| | | | | |

**Figure 10.3** Step 2 Input

but your passing game is very poor. You analyze your team's structure to see what things need to change so that the structure supports a passing game. For example, you may choose to beef up your offensive line so that you have strong protection for the quarterback, giving him plenty of time to pass. Organizationally, that might mean rotating offensive linemen frequently, so that they would not become fatigued. You might decide to negotiate a transfer of some defensive linemen into an offensive role. You may choose to have a wide variety of receivers available to catch a long ball, a short pass, and all varieties in between. From an organizational perspective, you may choose to rotate your receivers so that the defensive team cannot easily target one or two. All of the above choices represent ways that you might choose to change the offensive team's structure to support the new strategy.

Figure 10.4 depicts the relative value in the marketplace of certain roles and the degree of difficulty associated with gaining a particular skill. It's important to look at your talent from this perspective because it is directly related to your strategy for staffing your organization. Let's begin by looking at each role on your team, and deciding whether or not it is something you want to staff up for or outsource.

From Figure 10.4 can be inferred four guiding principles:

- If a skill has a long development cycle and adds little value—in other words, the skill is not a differentiator for your group—that skill should be outsourced versus hired.
- If a skill does not differentiate you but is easy to learn, then you can train existing employees.

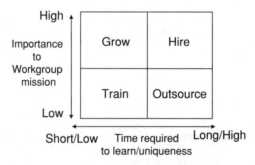

**Figure 10.4** Grow Talent vs. Buy Talent

- If a skill is moderately easy to train, but provides high value and differentiates you as a company, you should acquire this skill set, either by training existing employees or by hiring people with this capability.
- If a skill is relatively difficult to train, has a long development cycle, but is of high value in the marketplace, you should hire this skill.

*Step 3: Evaluate your current talent.* Once you have identified what you must do to be successful, and how you are going to organize to do it, look at the skills of the people you already have and determine whether they are sufficient to get the job done. At the same time, identify any areas that will need beefing up. In evaluating your current talent, we suggest you look at it from two perspectives:

- Employee relative contribution
- Employee growth potential

We will begin by considering the relative contribution of each of the employees in your workgroup. Not all employees' contribution to the company is the same. Applying the same strategy to finding and keeping all talent is overlooking a key element: contribution.

Figure 10.5 provides a way of thinking about the relative contribution of individual employees by placing them in different quadrants: Superstars, Heavy Hitters, Specialists, and Worker Bees. It is related to but not the same as the Buy versus Grow chart in Figure 10.4. Looking at someone's contribution to meeting your goal gives

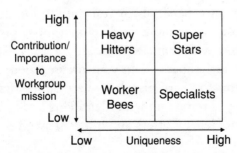

**Figure 10.5** Relative Contribution of Employees

| Staffing Plan | | | |
|---|---|---|---|
| Step 3: Evaluate your current talent. | | | |

| A. Evaluate employee contribution to goal attainment. | | | |
|---|---|---|---|
| Employee Name | Describe Contribution to Mission | Describe Uniqueness of Skills | Quadrant |
| Insert name here | | | Super Star, Heavy Hitter, Specialist, or Worker Bee |
| | | | |
| | | | |

| B. Consider employee growth potential | | | |
|---|---|---|---|
| Employee Name | Current Quadrant | Potential to Move To | Actions Needed |
| | | | |
| | | | |

**Figure 10.6**  Step 3 Input

you a critical view of the relative value of your team members. Figure 10.5 looks at employees from two perspectives: the uniqueness of their skills and their contribution to your mission.

- Superstars are people who possess unique skills and whose contribution to your goals is very high. If you were to calculate the value of this employee based on his or her contribution to the company, it would most likely be significantly higher than their overall compensation.
- An example of a Superstar might be the person responsible for the development of your leading technology product. Let's say there are only one or two people in the entire country who possess her combination of skill and program management capabilities. If you were to lose this person, it might cost you millions of dollars in missed opportunities, yet her compensation is significantly lower than this.
- You have few Superstars in your organization, if any. If you have them, they are priceless. Very aggressive tactics will be employed to retain them. Identifying and isolating Superstars from Heavy Hitters and others may give you the flexibility to do so.

- Heavy Hitters are big contributors, but they do not necessarily possess unique skills. Nevertheless, their value in the marketplace is very high. The Heavy Hitter in your organization might be the Sales VP who consistently delivers spectacular results. The skills are replaceable, but it would be a significant blow to the organization if they were to leave. Heavy Hitters, like Super Stars, are usually few in number. They are the yeast that makes the rest of the organization rise.

- Specialists are people with unique skills, difficult to replace on the market. They contribute to the company, but in a narrower way. Specialists may be few in number, but their contribution—although more narrowly focused—is very important. On the other hand, the bulk of your technical resources fall into the specialist category. Their value in the marketplace is a function of the demand for their particular skill.

- Worker Bees are people whose individual contributions to the company are neither high nor critical to your mission. These skills are more readily available on the open market. Like all employees, it is important to treat worker bees fairly. However, should a worker bee decide to leave, no heroic measures need be taken to retain them.

Next, look at the growth potential of your employees. Do any of your Specialists have the potential to become Superstars or Heavy Hitters? What about your Worker Bees? Are there individuals performing below their ability because they are not being challenged? What would it take for a Worker Bee to become a Specialist or a Heavy Hitter? Identify the people in your organization who have potential to increase the value of their contribution to the company, and the actions that would be needed to achieve their potential.

*Step 4: Plan for Succession.* Next, anticipate any openings that will occur in your organization due to promotions. Does an opening that you anticipate offer an opportunity to retain a talented but unchallenged employee who may be considering leaving?

**Staffing Plan**
*Step 4: Plan for succession.*

A. *Identify key vacancies in your workgroup/department/division/organization, by listing job titles in the appropriate blanks*

| Workgroup Openings | Department Openings | Division Openings | Organization Openings |
|---|---|---|---|
|  |  |  |  |
|  |  |  |  |
|  |  |  |  |

B. *Map current employees into potential openings*

| Job Title | Location | Candidate | Projected to Fill By |
|---|---|---|---|
|  |  |  |  |
|  |  |  |  |
|  |  |  |  |

C. *Identify vacancies created by employee promotions*

| Job Title | Location | Projected Date of Vacancy |
|---|---|---|
|  |  |  |
|  |  |  |
|  |  |  |

D. *Identify gaps to be sourced outside of company*

| Job Title | Number of Vacancies | Location | Date |
|---|---|---|---|
|  |  |  |  |
|  |  |  |  |

**Figure 10.7**   Step 4 Input

*Step 5: Anticipate attrition.* In this step you will identify employees who are thinking of leaving your group. Forecast who is likely to head for greener pastures, and what capabilities will go out the door with them. (In Chapter 17 we will discuss retention and

**Staffing Plan**
*Step 5: Anticipate attrition.*

ACTION:
Identify the employees that you feel may be considering leaving the company, indicating the value of their contribution (by quadrant) and anticipated attrition date.

| Employee | Role | Quadrant | Vulnerability Indicator | Projected Attrition Date |
|---|---|---|---|---|
|  |  |  |  |  |
|  |  |  |  |  |

**Figure 10.8**   Step 5 Input

| Staffing Plan |||
| :--- | :--- | :--- |
| *Step 6: Determine hiring specifications* |||
| ACTION: Prioritize the vacancies you would like to have filled by quarter. |||
| **Job Title** | **Number of Vacancies** | **Quarter to Fill** |
| | | |

**Figure 10.9**   Step 6 Input

turnaround tactics, but for now you're building a worst-case scenario.) The objective of attrition planning is to begin to source for these key positions before the loss occurs. By being proactive you can create a backlog of employees available to fill key roles as they become vacant, and save lost time.

*Step 6: Define hiring specifications.* Identify and prioritize the positions you would like to have filled within the next year. This chart should be updated on a quarterly basis. Having this information available will allow you to quickly identify to HR or staff recruiters the positions you want them to source.

*Step 7: Develop candidate sourcing strategy.* All companies are different, and each company has a unique value proposition that will allow it to compete effectively in the talent marketplace. Your sourcing strategy takes into consideration your culture, your budget, the type of resources you need to get the job done, and the constraints within which you must operate.

| Staffing Plan ||
| :--- | :--- |
| *Step 7: Develop candidate sourcing strategy* ||
| A. Bring forward culture description from Chapter 9, and identify your value proposition. ||
| **Culture Description** | **Value Proposition** |
| | |
| B. Identify any other constraints that will affect your ability to source. ||
| | |
| C. Based on your culture, value proposition, and other constraints, what will be your strategy for sourcing candidates? ||
| | |

**Figure 10.10**   Step 7 Input

## How to Fill Out the Staffing Plan

Instructions for completing the staffing plan are included in the form (Figure 10.11) which can be downloaded from *www. books.mcgraw-hill.com/training/download*. The staffing plan can become a part of your management process, to be reviewed on a regular basis with your management team. Included in the Appendix are two sample forms filled out by two different organizations: CYA Technologies, Inc., a software company that develops software products and utilities for Web content management systems, and the New Jersey State Police Mobile Data Computers project team.

| Staffing Plan Worksheet | | | | |
|---|---|---|---|---|

| Manager: | | Department: | | |
|---|---|---|---|---|

*Step 1: Understand the goals of your corporate strategy.*

ACTION: Identify the main goals of your corporate strategy:

| Goal ID | Corporate Goal Description | | | |
|---|---|---|---|---|
| | | | | |
| | | | | |

*Step 2: Describe your workgroup's goals and the structure you will need to achieve them.*

ACTIONS:
(A) List the goals of your workgroup in the column entitled "Workgroup Goal Description".
(B) List your plan to achieve each goal in the column entitled "Plan to Achieve".
(C) Insert or attach a copy of the proposed organization chart that you will use to achieve your goals.
(D) List the roles (Example: Project Manager) you will need in the column entitled "Identified Workgroup Roles", and identify whether you (1) already have them, (2) plan to grow them or (3) buy them in the appropriate columns.

| A. Workgroup Goal Description | | B. Plan to Achieve | | |
|---|---|---|---|---|
| | | | | |
| | | | | |

**C. Organization:**
   (Insert organization chart here.)

| D. Identified Workgroup Roles | Have | Grow | Outsource | Buy (Hire) |
|---|---|---|---|---|
| | | | | |

*Step 3:  Evaluate your current talent.*

A.  Evaluate employee contribution to goal attainment.

| Employee Name | Describe Contribution to Mission | Describe Uniqueness of Skills | Quadrant |
|---|---|---|---|
| Insert name here | | | Super Star, Heavy Hitter, Specialist, or Worker Bee |
| | | | |
| | | | |

B.  Consider employee growth potential

| Employee Name | Current Quadrant | Potential to Move To | Actions Needed |
|---|---|---|---|
| | | | |
| | | | |

*Step 4:  Plan for succession.*

A   Identify key vacancies in your workgroup/department/division/organization, by listing job titles in the appropriate blanks.

| Workgroup Openings | Department Openings | Division Openings | Organization Openings |
|---|---|---|---|
| | | | |
| | | | |
| | | | |

B.  Map current employees into potential openings

| Job Title | Location | Candidate | Projected to Fill By |
|---|---|---|---|
| | | | |
| | | | |
| | | | |

C.  Identify vacancies created by employee promotions

| Job Title | Location | Projected Date of Vacancy |
|---|---|---|
| | | |
| | | |
| | | |

D.  Identify gaps (vacancies) to be sourced from outside of company.

| Job Title | Number of Vacancies | Location | Date |
|---|---|---|---|
| | | | |
| | | | |
| | | | |

*Step 5:  Anticipate attrition.*

ACTION:
Identify the employees that you feel may be considering leaving the company, indicating the value of their contribution (by quadrant) and anticipated attrition date.

| Employee | Role | Quadrant | Vulnerability Indicator | Projected Attrition Date |
|---|---|---|---|---|
| | | | | |
| | | | | |
| | | | | |

*Step 6: Determine hiring specifications*

ACTION: Prioritize the vacancies you would like to have filled by quarter.

| Job Title | Number of Vacancies | Quarter to Fill |
|---|---|---|
|  |  |  |

*Step 7: Develop candidate sourcing strategy*

A. Bring forward culture description from Chapter 9, and identify your value proposition.

| Culture Description | Value Proposition |
|---|---|
|  |  |

B. Identify any other constraints that will affect your ability to source.

|  |
|---|
|  |

C. Based on your culture, value proposition, and other constraints, what will be your strategy for sourcing candidates?

|  |
|---|
|  |

**Figure 10.11**   Staffing Plan Worksheet

# 11

# How to Create an "Ideal Hire" Profile

ARE YOU REALLY LOOKING for a candidate who knows C++, or are you looking for someone who can think critically? The match between the employee and the company goes beyond the technology. And most people think of "most qualified" as applying only to technology. Most qualified really includes the skills, culture, values, and work to be accomplished. It does no good to hire a "lone ranger" if in fact you need a "team player." And hiring the wrong person can be the most costly decision you'll ever make.

Table 11.1 below is an example of an Ideal Hire Profile for a position. This chapter describes how to create an Ideal Hire

**Table 11.1** Ideal "Hire Profile"

| Position | Software Engineer | | | |
|---|---|---|---|---|
| Selection Criterion | Must Have | Must Have | Nice to Have | Nice to Have |
| Character | | | | |
| Culture | | | | |
| Capabilities | | | | |

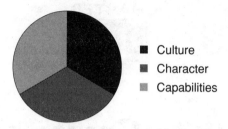

**Figure 11.1**  Culture Profile

Profile for a given job that allows you to focus your interview on selecting potential employees for the qualities that will be most important to you. In this chapter we differentiate desirable qualities from must-haves, and describe how to tell the difference. There are qualities you'll never find on a resumé, and a 30-minute interview won't reveal them either, but they're as important to your success as technology skills. In this chapter we will explore the topic of employee selection from the perspective of: Culture, Character, and Capabilities.

Don't overlook any of these elements when you're hiring. Each of these elements is equally important and hiring priorities for individual positions will differ for each company and each position.

### Character

Character shows up in how a person relates to, and interacts with, others and their environment. It is developed throughout a lifetime, and is shaped by one's values, upbringing, experiences, and other life influences. It is honed by adversity, and can be observed in the decisions a person makes about his or her conduct. Adversity is the crucible in which character is hardened. It is for this reason that many successful search executives will not consider for a major role an individual who has not experienced failure. Failure is a great teacher. Many personal characteristics are subsumed into character, including courage, candor, and integrity. This is the most important selection factor. Without character, it doesn't really matter how good an individual is technically: their technical value will be obscured by their lack of character. Character, seen in action, energizes a company. It can be seen in the person who takes a difficult stand because it's the right thing to do, the person who is consistently on time for appointments, the person who meets commitments and deadlines.

The converse of this is the person who always blames others for his or her failings. People of character are accountable. They make mistakes, like others, but they'll never hide them or surprise you with them. Consequently, character breeds trust and stability in a company. It engenders respect from clients and employees. In Chapter 14 we provide specific interview techniques that will help you select for character.

The CEO of a technology company, complained in an interview "I know that if I am not there and a client problem surfaces at an odd hour, there are probably no more than two percent of my current employees I can trust to hang in there and solve the problem." The others would leave and go home to do whatever it is that they do. She hasn't been selecting for character, and it impacts her ability to grow the companies. If she cannot replicate her dedication and sense of responsibility to clients, it means that she must continually be dragged into solving customer problems, instead of growing the companies.

## Culture

The Culture Profile you developed in Chapter 9 will become part of your Ideal Hire Profile. As you develop your Ideal Hire Profile, the culture element will most likely remain constant in all of your Ideal Hire Profiles. However, if you are recruiting for a department or division whose culture may be different from the rest of the corporation, you may want to re-examine the culture profile. (An example may be an IT function in a technology-dependent company. The level of stress and results emphasis might be different, and would need to be taken into consideration when staffing.)

**Table 11.2** Four Basic Capabilities

| Learning | Analyzing | Relating | Performing |
|---|---|---|---|
| Active learning | Technical Acumen | Perceptiveness | Sense of Urgency |
| Knowledge Transfer | Business Acumen | Influence | Execution |
| Developing Others | Problem Solving | Collaboration | Drive to Achieve |
| | Decisiveness | Customer Insight | Accomplishment Optimism |

## Capabilities

We have grouped the basic employee capabilities into the table in Table 11.2. Under each capability we have identified specific traits or skills that can be observed and measured by how individuals behave, the work they do, and the decisions they make. The remainder of this chapter looks more deeply at these capabilities and how they shape performance.

In order to effectively compare employees, you need to have a common frame of reference. Our model serves as a benchmark and allows you to determine the traits your tech resources need to succeed. It will help you identify potential and existing employees' strengths and weaknesses. We suggest you use it:

- To create a dialogue with recruiters, Human Resources, or managers about selecting resources
- To create a common language for discussing individual development needs
- As a guide for succession planning
- In professional growth discussions with direct reports or manager

## Learning

Learning measures a person's receptivity to new information, and the level and speed with which they can absorb complexity. Learning is the "engine" that fuels the ongoing development of a person. In the technology industry, the speed of change means that languages learned six months ago may be obsolete today.

The key Learning skills are:

- *Active Learning.* The active learner proactively seeks out experiences that are likely to improve skills. The active learner has a passion for technology and can quickly absorb and assimilate a large amount of information.
- *Knowledge Transfer* measures a willingness to translate experiences into knowledge gained for the organization. The person who is good at knowledge transfer will help an organization grow. Knowledge Transfer is a particularly important skill for a manager or mentor to possess.
- *Developing Others* measures a willingness to openly share information with others in order to improve individual performance. The person who is good at developing others willingly teaches, coaches, or mentors others to more effective modes of operation, a skill that is invaluable in building an organization.

Learning can be observed using test instruments, multi-rater feedback instruments, simulations, and the Behavioral Interview. In Chapter 14 we describe how to interview for Learning and other capabilities.

People who are strong learners will be thought leaders in your company. The ability to stay abreast of—or ahead of—changes in technology are reflected in how well a company learns. Strong learners not only teach themselves, but will use their ability to raise the water level throughout your organization.

### Analyzing

Analyzing measures depth and breadth of a person's technical knowledge; their ability to think critically, solve problems rapidly, and make sound business decisions. Skilled analytics are able to anticipate the effects of their decisions and actions. Analyzing allows the individual to manage and adapt to both ambiguity and complexity. Most technical people are strong analytically, but may exhibit different skill strengths.

Analyzing consists of four skills:

- *Technical Acumen* measures the breadth and depth of a person's technical knowledge. This skill differs substantially for every company, and takes into consideration the unique technical skills required to achieve each company's mission. When selecting for technical acumen, the Ideal Hire Profile would specify both the technology and the level of skill desired.
- *Business Acumen* measures the knowledge and understanding of how business processes work and how value is created. Business acumen includes understanding both the scope and risk associated with the work at hand. Program Managers, Business and Operations Managers usually have business acumen. It is accumulated over time through experience.
- *Problem Solving* measures the ability to apply critical thinking to analyze relevant information and identify practical and applicable solutions to everyday business problems. Strength in Problem Solving will distinguish the Systems Analyst or Technical Problem Solver from others. Problem Solving should be a selection criterion wherever critical thinking is paramount.
- *Decision Making* measures the understanding of cause-and-effect relationships between actions and intended result. Strong decision makers are not afraid to make a decision with less-than-perfect information. In doing so, they consider both obvious and unintended consequences. Decision Making is often a management selection criterion. It is especially important in Program and Project Management.

Technical Acumen can be seen in the person's work outputs and the observations of others. In Chapter 15 we offer specific suggestions on how to evaluate technical ability. Problem Solving and Decision Making in action can be demonstrated through simulations. It is possible to assess technical acumen during the interview process itself. (This topic is expanded in Chapters 14—Interview tactics that leave no wiggle room, and 15—How to Conduct the Technical Depth Drill).

Bridget O'Connor, Senior Vice President of Information Technology for Lehman Brothers, when asked about her biggest hiring mistake in her career indicated, "I hired a fellow who had a 'reputation' regarding a single technology. I assumed he was open-minded. I put him in charge of a unit that had responsibility for a different technology. During the interview, he said all the right things. However, in practice, he was very single-minded and required more management oversight to keep him open-minded than I either had time for or anticipated."

O'Connor was looking for not only technical competence. She needed it packaged with good business acumen. She needed someone who understood that the solution to the problem was a business solution as much as a technical one. Once viewed from this perspective, it becomes clear that the solution was not to scrap a multi-million dollar investment in one technology to solve the problem. Viewed from a technical perspective, the problem seemed like one technology approach and its merits versus another. Viewed from a business perspective, the problem was "How do I maximize my existing investment?"

## Relating

Relating looks at how well people understand and interact with others, and measures their ability to predict the affect of their actions on others. Relating requires empathy. It is the glue that holds an organization together, cements customer relations, and allows people to work effectively with and among others. Important in every culture, it is especially important in a Lifestyle culture.

The key skills that are aspects of Relating are:

- *Perceptiveness* measures the ability to assess and respond to both verbal and non-verbal cues from others. The perceptive person will understand and empathize with others. They can make a "connection" easily with customers and co-workers.
- *Influence* measures the ability to change the behavior and thinking of others through persuasion. The strong influencer is a good communicator who conveys a convincing, professional

demeanor in all situations. Influence is usually a selection criterion in a sales role.

- *Collaboration* measures a person's ability to work constructively with others. Collaboration is a must in any organization that works together as teams. Project teams, for example, need collaborative working environments. Collaboration should be a selection criterion whenever teamwork is essential.
- *Customer Insight* measures how well a person relates to and understands the customer. The person with good customer insight makes business decisions that support the customer's objectives.

People who are good at relating make excellent sales or customer support personnel. The ability to view a situation from a customer's perspective will go a long way toward establishing good customer relationships. They tend to form kind of partnerships that immunize them to competitive pressure. Sensitivity to others makes one a caring, supportive manager.

Relating can be observed as people interact with one another in real or simulated situations, through multi-rater feedback, and the Behavioral Interview.

Bob Russell, Chief Operating Officer for Thomson Industries, "...wants more team players than superstars. Superstars need a little special care and feeding. And if this special handling is not done well, it can be a detriment to the rest of the organization."

Russell, known for creating high performing teams, looks for individuals who not only possess good business acumen, but also people who work together collaboratively. This formula has been a success for him and makes for a good fit in his culture.

## Performance

Performance describes how a person uses action to achieve results. It is the engine that drives sales and impacts the bottom line more directly than most other capabilities.

Key aspects of Performance are:

- *Sense of Urgency* measures whether a person approaches work with energy and intensity to completion. The person with a strong sense of urgency is focused on getting the job done, and tends to prioritize action over deliberation.

- *Execution* describes how a person goes about achieving results. The person who is good at execution not only gets the job done, but also builds relationships in the process. This person will consider objectives beyond their own, and if necessary, sacrifice personal achievement for the good of the organization.
- *Accomplishment* measures consistency in meeting one's goals. Does the person meet their goals consistently? Do they overachieve them? Do they take pleasure in performing?
- *Optimism.* The optimist views events and failures as temporary setbacks, persevering until results are achieved. The optimistic person will reframe events until they identify the things they can change or control, and not let adverse circumstances immobilize or demoralize them.

Performance can be seen in a list of accomplishments in a resumé, through a Behavioral Interview, through multi-rater feedback and personality instruments, and through direct observation of behavior in either a real or simulated situation.

Strong performers are generally self-starters. You will see them taking initiative and focusing on results. They have a bias toward action, and can generally be counted on to get the job done. The best ones do so without stepping on others in the process. In fact, they might sacrifice a personal goal for the greater good of the organization. Select leaders, Program Managers, and sales for Performance.

### Hiring criteria

Whether you're staffing a project, a client engagement, or an internal position, some characteristics of the individual will be more important than others. When evaluating a potential hire, consider Character, Culture, and Capabilities—which include the work and the environment in which it is created. The most common reasons for failure have less to do with technical competence and more to do with a poor fit with the culture. Therefore, one of the things that comes to the top of a selection model is compatibility with the culture.

Clearly define your culture, your values, and the things that are important to you. Don't be nice. Be honest. Don't define what you would like it to be. Be brutally frank about what it is.

Look at the people who are successful. What characteristics do they have in common? You can't effectively sell your company to a prospective hire until you can describe it accurately. And tell them what kind of a person is happy there.

If you've followed the suggestions offered in Chapter 9, you have described a culture fit. What else should you select for? And how?

The ideal hire profile looks at how to prioritize the skills most important to you. Selecting for too many things defeats the purpose of developing an ideal hire profile. With every additional selection criterion you add, you narrow the pool of eligibles. The goal is to keep selection criteria to a minimum. Conversely, selecting for the wrong things can be deadly. When hiring a technical person, for example, a common assumption is that one should select for languages, or other technical abilities. Without understanding what their goals will be, you may be selecting for something that is relatively easy to develop and missing something that has a much longer development time. Critical thinking and business acumen take years to develop. On the other hand, facility with a particular programming language can be learned in weeks.

Simply dumping the sourcing and screening of candidates to HR is a losing proposition. Field managers must be involved in partnership with HR in the sourcing, interviewing, and screening of candidates. It is the line managers who can make the "connection" with potential hires. Talent attracts talent, and talented employees are looking at those interviewing them with the same critical eye that the interviewer uses. They don't feel as if they need to impress the interviewer. Quite the contrary. The interviewer needs to excite and impress them with the work they will be doing, the quality of the leadership team, the culture and vision of the company, and the specific opportunities that exist.

### Conclusion

This chapter has streamlined your hiring process and provided clarity about what to select for, so that you can make rapid, sound decisions about potential hires. We know that there is a scarcity of resources out there, but that doesn't mean that you shouldn't be selective. As we were conducting our research an interesting fact kept cropping up. *People who were experiencing a lot of employee turnover reported that being more selective in the hiring process actually resulted in reduced employee turnover. Whereas, people who are simply trying to bring in warm bodies reported that they often fill the same position as many as four times in a given year.*

# Five "Must Have" Roles for a Good Project Team

IF FITTING A CANDIDATE into a particular project team isn't an issue for you, skip this chapter. But if you're filling out an existing work group or creating a new one from scratch, here's where you'll find out how to combine different capabilities for a productive, cohesive team.

Every IT department must fill five roles to succeed. Some roles are crucial at the earliest stages of the company's growth; others come into play a little later. Some can be outsourced; others can't. But the right mix is essential.

This chapter shows how to identify those five types when they walk through your door, and more important, what to do with them after that. We've given them names: Ice Breaker, Sherlock, Straw Boss, Guru, and Sherpa.

Before looking at each type, it's important to point out a fundamental difference in technology developers—"wide bodies" versus "tall bodies".

As Figure 12.1 shows, different people take different paths. Wide bodies develop functional knowledge in a variety of areas; tall bodies develop technical depth in a specific area. Keep this distinction in mind as you look at each type.

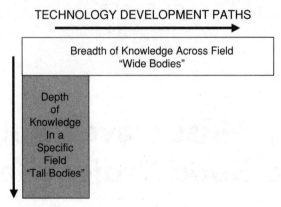

**Figure 12.1** Wide Bodies vs. Tall Bodies

- *Ice Breaker:* The individual that can break down the doors and create opportunities for the company. Technically, a wide body.
- *Sherlock:* The critical thinker. The systems analyst or problem solver. A wide body.
- *Straw Boss:* The person who can lead a project, program team, product group, or company to success. A wide body.
- *Guru:* The acknowledged expert in a particular technology. A tall body.
- *Sherpa:* The backbone of any organization, the worker bee. Technically functional in a given technology. May become either a wide body or a tall body, with development.

### Ice Breaker

In every company there's someone who creates the opportunity. The Ice Breaker is that person. An ideal solutions architect or technical sales person, the Ice Breaker can relate well with customers at all levels. Excellent communicators, they can easily reach a "meeting of the minds" with a customer, use their technical ability to synthesize customer needs into possible solutions, and accurately size or scope the project.

To look for Ice Breakers, pose customer problems and see how candidates approach the situation. Are they precise in their communication skills? Can they simplify technical concepts enough for a non-technical person to understand them? Do they grasp the business ramifications of the problem? Look for behavior designed to clarify concepts and confirm mutual understanding. A good Ice Breaker leads toward a solution, but never pushes.

In an internal IT department, the Ice Breaker is the person who interfaces with the end users to understand needs and propose solutions.

### Selecting Ice Breakers

Select an Ice Breaker for

- *Performance* (drive to achieve): The Ice Breaker is responsible for bringing business in the door. You want people who approach their work with energy and intensity all the way to completion. Goal orientation is important, but the way Ice Breakers go about achieving their goals is just as important. Look for consistent achievers who also work cooperatively with others. They need to be resilient, willing to take rejection and persevere until the goal is attained.
- *Influence*: Ice Breakers are your chief communicators. It is important that they can clearly and forcefully convey information to others. In the tech world this means listening as well as speaking. The Ice Breaker must bring the client to agreement about the specifics of the solution and the functionality that will be delivered. This requires good interactive skills, excellent probing skills, and clarity of thought and expression.
- *Business Acumen*: The Ice Breaker must be able to understand and effectively assess risk in programs and develop contingencies to offset them. The good Ice Breaker understands that both revenue generation and risk reduction impact the bottom line. You want the Ice Breaker to understand the business ramifications of the solution/s they are responsible for selling.
- *Customer Insight*: As the primary point of contact with the customer, the Ice Breaker clearly understands the customer,

the customer's strategy, and how your solution adds value. Decisions should reflect this focus on client satisfaction. The best Ice Breakers will be perceived by the client as a business partner and will be included in key meetings and invited to discuss strategic issues. The more competitive the situation, the lower the level of perceived partnership between the Ice Breaker and the client.

### Contributions to the Team

- Performance, measured in client satisfaction or in meeting sales goals, is what drives the Ice Breaker. He or she will deliver the business needed to keep the company functioning.
- Good Ice Breakers know enough technically to understand the limitations of their technology and not over-promise on capabilities.
- Good Ice Breakers can communicate effectively with the Gurus, Straw Bosses, and Sherlocks to shape the design of a solution.
- The best Ice Breakers can work well with all members of a project team, both internal and external, balancing all needs effectively.

### Potential Blind Sides or Development Needs

- If they are not technically strong or balanced with a technically strong person, they may overpromise on technology or overcommit on deadlines.
- A by-product of their drive to perform might be an insensitivity to others on the project team. They might unintentionally overlook the impact of their actions on others.

### The Sherlock

The Sherlock is the position most frequently mis-hired. Recruiters are often dazzled by the technical expertise of the individual and overlook the main reason for hiring this person: he or she is the critical thinker whose job it is to analyze the issues, dissect them ruthlessly, and solve them quickly. Sherlocks are strong on analytical talent and can absorb a lot of material quickly. They are nothing if not a quick study. Sherlocks get bored with problems that are "old hat."

Don't ask about programming languages. They are irrelevant. Give these candidates simulations that test their problem solving skills and watch how they approach the situation. Good Sherlock candidates will ask lots of questions. Don't spend your time waiting for their answer: simply observe their process.

### Selecting Sherlocks

Select a Sherlock for:

- *Technical Breadth* (wide body): Your Sherlock is your problem solver, your critical thinker. You would like to be able to leverage this expertise across multiple opportunities, so you are looking for someone who knows a lot about multiple technologies. They may be a designated expert in a specific technology, but they also possess functional knowledge in a broad array of technologies. It is not the depth of this person's knowledge that will solve the problem. Rather, it is the way they approach it.
- *Active learning*: Sherlocks thrive on ambiguity and paradox. They actively seek new learning opportunities and quickly see parallels between seemingly disparate events. They tend to be insightful about their own strengths and weaknesses, and are constantly striving to improve themselves.
- *Problem solving*: The Sherlock has the ability to see the "entire" problem. He or she searches for and finds multiple solutions. Sherlocks are able to distinguish the "best" approach from multiple alternatives and see the ramifications of alternate solutions, especially those that are not immediately obvious. Their problem-solving process includes mechanisms to uncover creative alternatives.
- *Knowledge transfer*: The Sherlock collects, solicits, and disseminates knowledge as necessary to help others in his/her group. He or she routinely conducts project postmortems in

the spirit of continuous improvement, and uses appropriate group methods to catalog and share experiences.

## Contributions to the Team

- Challenges the status quo. Questions accepted facts. Forces a team to think deeply about issues.
- Helps explore and imagine alternatives—either as solutions to problems or as approaches to designing products.
- Can turn analysis into action.
- Helps an organization grow through development of competencies.
- Can be an excellent mentor.

## Blind Spots or Development Needs

- The Sherlock approaches life from a thinking perspective, and in doing so may be insensitive to the needs of others.
- Sherlocks sometimes need to improve their communication skills. At times the knowledge gap between Sherlocks and those they interact with is so wide that they have difficulty bridging it.
- The Sherlock enjoys the intellectual challenge of the problem, and likes to try multiple alternatives in seeking the optimum solution. He or she may need to develop a greater sense of urgency to solve the problem at hand.

## The Straw Boss

The Straw Boss can lead a project, program team, product group, or company to success. People enjoy working for—and with—this person. Straw Bosses have a strong focus on performance, get along well with others, and are tuned into the customer and the marketplace.

The key to the success of the Straw Boss is good balance among all of the capabilities. Natural leaders, Straw Bosses tend to be very forceful and focused on goal attainment. They have a very balanced profile and typically have moved up through the ranks within an organization. Their skills are such that they are capable of stepping into any of the other roles, should the need arise.

In smaller companies the Straw Boss tends to be a role played by an individual who is also producing product. In larger companies and in larger projects, Straw Boss becomes a full-time occupation. In an internal IT department, the Straw Boss is a project manager who moves from one implementation to another.

One example of a Straw Boss is the program manager on a large systems integration project. This person fills a "start-up CEO" role at the beginning of the program, obtains capital funding, staffs up the organization, and leads the design team in product design. Then the Straw Boss assumes the role of VP of manufacturing while the program team goes about the process of developing the solution to meet the client's needs.

All the while, the Straw Boss is interacting with the other members of the program team and the client team to assure that communications are clear and that the project is moving along according to schedule. The Straw Boss must assess, quantify, and manage risk while balancing the needs of the client and the company. So, in doing so, the Straw Boss is exercising good management skills, good leadership skills, good communication skills, and good process and project management skills.

### Selecting Straw Bosses

Select Straw Bosses for the following capabilities:

- *Business Acumen*: The Straw Boss has a general manager's understanding of how business processes and functions interrelate. He or she can create a comprehensive, well-crafted business plan and is able to assess and mitigate program risks. The Straw Boss understands how his/her company's ability to create value relates to the overall health of the industry. This person also understands that both revenue generation and risk reduction impact the bottom line and consequently focuses on both revenue generation as well as risk reduction opportunities. A pragmatist, the Straw Boss draws distinctions between textbook and real-world systems and processes.

- *Decision Making*: The Straw Boss appropriately balances the need for sufficient information with the need to act. He or she makes timely decisions that take plausible cause and effect relationships into account. Straw Bosses anticipate reactions of others and plan accordingly. They are nothing if not decisive, and will break a tie to keep the group on task.
- *Relating*: The Straw Boss interacts with clients, team members, and others in the company. Good relating skills are essential. The Straw Boss clearly and forcefully communicates to others in a way that tends to influence their thinking. S/he makes a powerful impact. The Straw Boss works constructively with others to accomplish a task.
- *Performance*: The Straw Boss approaches work with energy and intensity to completion. S/he takes actions on those items where one can have clear and observable impact. The Straw Boss possesses solid process management skills and gets the job done, on time and on specification.

### Contributions to the Organization

- Drives teams to work productively and profitably.
- Very process oriented. Thinks in terms of milestones and meeting deadlines.
- Decisive. The Straw Boss will stop debate and make a decision to move the ball forward.
- Good Straw Bosses will drive organizational learning by developing the members of their program teams.
- They make excellent mentors.

### Blind Spots or Development Needs

- Because Straw Bosses *are* so focused on performance, they may run over others in getting the job done.

### The Guru

Gurus are designated experts in a specific technology. Their range of knowledge may be fairly narrow, but in that field, they rule.

Gurus revel in a technical challenge, and enjoy being asked to solve difficult problems in their field of expertise. They care less about expanding the breadth of their expertise than becoming more proficient in a given area. Their strongest area is analyzing.

Gurus are respected by other technologists, who look to them as mentors. Their ability to communicate with executives may be limited. Their love of the technology and "how the watch was made" tends to influence their communication skills. Pair them effectively with an Ice Breaker when dealing with customers.

## Selecting Gurus

Select Gurus for:

- *Technical Acumen* (depth): The Guru is an acknowledged expert in a given technology. S/he probably has a reputation for competence in this area.
- *Problem Solving*: Gurus thrive on complexity, ambiguity and paradox. The more difficult the problem, the more satisfaction they will derive from solving it. They actively seek new learning opportunities and quickly see parallels between seemingly disparate events. Although the Sherlock also thrives on solving complex problems, the difference with the Guru is that the problems are confined to an area where they are technically deep.
- *Active Learning*: Gurus continually challenge and evolve their own mental models. They seek unknown areas as a basis for increasing their depth of knowledge in a chosen field. Gurus may prefer working on many projects and problems at once. They quickly find parallels and connections among disparate events or perspectives.

## Contributions to the Team

- Brings depth and range to the exploration of a problem.
- Increases the level of knowledge in the organization.
- Brings tremendous credibility in a given field. Makes a great expert presenter.
- Interfaces well with tech experts in client organizations.

### Blind Spots or Development Needs

- May be parochial in their approach to solving the problem. They will lead with their area of expertise.
- This is a hammer looking for a nail.
- May overcommunicate to the customer, giving a level of technical detail that while fascinating to them, is boring to the customer.

### The Sherpa

Sherpa are doers rather than managers of work. The typical Sherpa may be a software engineer with 18 to 20 years of experience or a new college graduate. What distinguishes Sherpas is their enjoyment of the actual creation of the product.

Individual profiles of the Sherpa vary, although the level of depth or breadth of proficiency or experience is the most likely differentiator. Given a profile as varied as this, it is important to understand the career goals of each Sherpa.

An early-career Sherpa will need career guidance to what work they really want to do. Sherpas are the backbone of any organization. They may be new to IT, a budding Guru, Ghostbuster, Straw Boss or Ice Breaker, or they may just be an individual who delights in learning new technology. These are the people who get the job done on a daily basis. Treasure them.

### Selecting Sherpas

Select Sherpas for

- Technical Acumen (functional): Sherpas work effectively as members of a project team under specific direction. They can design and develop programs of acceptable quality unassisted. They usually know several programming languages, and are proficient at them. They may, however, require assistance when working complex problems.
- Collaboration: Sherpas work constructively and cooperatively with others in accomplishing a task. They adopt a "one for all" approach to work, and are good team players.

## Contributions to the Team

- Sherpas form the bulk of either a project team or a technical work force. They are the gals and guys who get the job done.
- They are the greatest contributors to the culture of the company, simply because of their sheer numbers.
- Innovation and new thinking. Sherpas, many of whom are new college graduates, bring new ways of doing and seeing things. This makes for innovation.

## Blind Spots or Development Needs

- Inexperience is a two-edged sword. It brings with it the fresh perspective that leads to breakthrough thinking. It also brings a vulnerability due to lack of experience.
- New Sherpas may be "building their resumé." Either they will get to do it with you, or you will be a stop on the road.
- Need career guidance. Sherpas who aren't talking to you about their careers don't see one with your company. Try to understand where they want to be from a knowledge and skills standpoint in the next two years. Then figure out how to make that happen with your company.

# 13

# How to Evaluate a Technical Resumé and Prepare for the Interview

BRIAN WILCOX IS GETTING READY to interview for some open positions in his department. He has three resumés that he likes for the role of Solutions Architect, and plans to interview three of the candidates tomorrow. It's 6:30 p.m., and he'd rather be on his way home to see his wife and children. It's been a long week already, what with the problem that popped up in the network... But, he would like to use the resumés to plan for his interviews. The goal of this chapter is to teach you how to use the resumé as a starting point to plan for an effective interview.

Following is a brief summary of the resumés together with a copy of the "ideal hire Profile for the Solutions Architect position. (See Chapter 11 to learn how to create an "ideal hire" profile.)

What do the resumés really tell him? And how much should he trust the information contained in a resumé? With the tremendous demand for technical resources, and with the search engines only

**Resumé and Ideal Hire Profile Comparison**

*Resumé No. 1:*                                                   *Ideal Hire Profile*

| |
|---|

**Sue Egabyte**

- Ten years' experience as Software Engineer and team lead in a series of mid-size companies
- B.S. Computer Science from Carnegie-Mellon University, 1991

**Operating Systems:**
Windows 95/98/2000, Sun Solaris, H-P UX

**Languages:**
C++, ColdFusion, HTML, Javascript

- Led a team tasked with providing IVAS enhancements and customized solutions for a mid-sized company. Under my leadership the team wrote and enhanced a complex EDI solution and other complex customized solutions for this company.
- Seven years' experience with one company. Career progression shows positions of increased responsibility.

**Must Haves:**

- Dependability
- Collaboration
- Java, C++, XML, Internet-based project experience
- Rational Rose or similar tools
- Influence
- Critical Thinking
- Business Acumen

**Nice to Have:**

- Problem Solving
- Drive to Achieve
- Active Learning
- Customer Insight

**Figure 13.1**  Resumé No. 1 and Ideal Hire Profile Comparison

picking up resumés that have key words in them, a significant number of applicants have in some way embellished their resumés. Today, it is assumed that most resumés (94%, in fact) falsely claim things like college degrees, list false employers, or identify jobs that did not exist. A resumé may list an incorrect job title, or misrepresent the reasons why a person left a particular employer, and roughly 1/3 of the resumés list dates of employment that are off by more than three months[1]. The resumé is only the starting point in understanding a candidate. At its most honest, a resumé represents an individual's perception of himself. That perception may or may not be accurate.

---

[1]In conducting research for this book we observed a number of technical interviews. Candidates disclosed to us that their previous managers routinely "embellished" their resumés when sending them on client engagements.

Brian begins his analysis by charting the career progression of the people based on their career history in the resumé. In so doing, he is trying to understand whether or not their experience warrants the type of position and salary range the open requisition requires. The resumé is an incomplete picture of each person, so he tries to mentally fill in the blanks as he studies each person's information. As he does so, he uses the ideal hire profile developed for this position. He reviews the candidates' resumés against the ideal hire profile to plan his interview of each of the three candidates: Sue, Byron and Patel. Later in this chapter we'll generate a

## Resumé and Ideal Hire Profile Comparison

| Resumé No. 2: | Ideal Hire Profile |
|---|---|
| **Patel Kernel** | **Must Haves:** |
| • Bachelor of Technology, Indian Institute of Technology, 1980 | • Dependability |
| **Operating Systems:** OS/2, Windows 95/98/NT, WSOD, and UNIX | • Collaboration |
| | • Java, C++, XML, Internet-based project experience |
| **Languages:** Java, C++, Pascal, JavaScript, and HTML | • Rational Rose or similar tools |
| **Networks:** NT, Novell, OS2 WarpServer, and Banyan | • Influence |
| • Experience with PVCS | • Critical Thinking |
| • Has managed a team of nine software engineers in all phases of both project and personnel management. | • Business Acumen |
| • Has worked as an applications development QE Manager, responsible for quality assurance on public set of software developed with Java APIs | **Nice to Have:** • Problem Solving • Drive to Achieve • Active Learning • Customer Insight |
| • Coordinated testing efforts and scheduled with development and QE engineers globally, including outsourced programming sites in Bulgaria and Beijing | |
| • Experience as a Compatibility Manager, assuring the compatibility of the software programs with a number of computer platforms, printer drivers, video display adapters, font rendering software, and network operating systems | |

**Figure 13.2**   Resumé No. 2 and Ideal Hire Profile Comparison

---

**Resumé and Ideal Hire Profile Comparison**

| *Resumé No. 3:* | *Ideal Hire Profile* |
|---|---|

**Byron Bits**

* Ten years experience in the computer industry
* Began his career as a writer of software documentation
* B.A. in English and Psychology
* Certificate in Computer Science, 1992

**Languages:**
Java, HTML, CGI Scripts, ActiveX, and incorporation of plug-ins such as Adobe Acrobat and Distiller

* 1993: WebMaster/Content Producer for large telecommunications company
* 1998: Consultant, working with large telecommunications companies, building Extranets and supporting large global web sites
* Last year: Became certified in XML
* Current: Project Manager with a dot com company, leading a team responsible for developing new content, applications, and data processes for a web site that changes hourly

**Must Haves:**
* Dependability
* Collaboration

* Java, C++, XML, Internet-based project experience
* Rational Rose or similar tools
* Influence
* Critical Thinking
* Business Acumen

**Nice to Have:**
* Problem Solving
* Drive to Achieve
* Active Learning
* Customer Insight

**Figure 13.3**   Resumé No. 3 and Ideal Hire Profile Comparison

list of fact-finding questions that Brian will use in the interview process. Table 13.1 shows how the selection criteria identified in the Ideal Hire Profile tie to the 3C's of selection: Character, Culture, and Capabilities.

**Table 13.1**   Ideal Hire Profile

| Position | Solutions Architect | | | |
|---|---|---|---|---|
| Selection Criterion | Must Have | Must Have | Nice to Have | Nice to Have |
| Character | Integrity | Dependability | Courage | |
| Culture (Lifestyle/Process) | Collaboration | Rational Rose or similar tools | | |
| Capabilities | Java, C++, XML Internet-based project experience | Critical Thinking | Problem Solving Drive to Achieve | Active Learning |
| | Influence | Business Acumen | Customer Insight | |

### Steps to effectively reviewing a resumé

- *Look at each position title the person has held*, and attempt to infer from the title the skills the person must have. Sue is a "Team Lead," Patel has managed a team, and Byron is a "Project Manager." All titles suggest responsibility for people and meeting deadlines. Each of those assumptions would lead to additional questions that could be asked to clarify the scope of the person's responsibility.
- *Develop a graph of the person's career history*, attempting to see his or her career progression. This will give you an indication of the level of technical breadth and depth, as well as tell you whether or not their career path has suffered any bumps along the way.

Let's look at the career progression of two different candidates: Byron and Patel.

Figure 13.4 is an example of a career progression chart for Byron. Byron started out with a degree in English and began his career as a technical writer. His first job title listed on the resumé was Software Documentation Specialist. His career path was fairly level for about seven years. During that time Byron began to expand his skills to include graphic design and the creation of

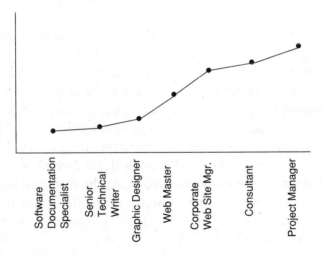

**Figure 13.4**  Career Progression—Brian

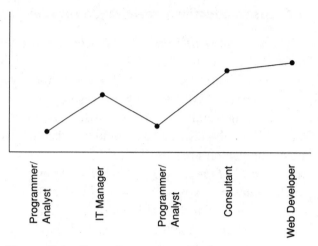

**Figure 13.5** Career Progression—Patel

Web sites. In his eighth year he was given a position as Web Master, having learned a number of HTML web authoring tools, forms and CGI scripts, graphics, animated GIFs, and other multimedia effects. He then became a Corporate Web Site Master, responsible for overseeing the construction of a large corporate web site. Subsequent to that, Byron added to his skills and, working as a consultant, developed an extranet for a large, global customer. Further building on his supervisory skills, Byron assumed the role of Project Manager for a mid-sized company.

- The second chart shows Patel's career progression. He began his career as a Programmer/Analyst, then was promoted into the role of IT Manager. Later, deciding that his skills were becoming obsolete, Patel took a backward step and became a Programmer/Analyst again in order to become trained on the newer languages, JAVA, C++, HTML. He then did some independent consulting as a web developer, and eventually took a job with his current employer as a Web Developer. So, in Patel's case the backward step indicates a sacrifice he was willing to make to improve his skills. This decision may reflect strength of character, and a willingness to take risks.

- *Map the candidate's skills with the selection profile.* Where are the strengths? Where are there potential gaps? What questions will you need to ask to clarify this? Let's look at how Brian's analysis of his candidates brings additional insight into their relative strengths. Table 13.2 examines how each candidate's resumé matches to the specific traits identified in the ideal hire profile and suggests areas where further information is required.

As he reviews each of the applicants and how they compare to the selection criteria, Brian first looks horizontally at each of the criteria, without evaluating the candidates individually. This horizontal focus keeps him from jumping to a conclusion based on an immediate first impression.

From a Character standpoint, dependability may be inferred based on a number of factors: (a) The average number of years the individual has stayed with one company, and (b) The level of progression each applicant has experienced—either with the same company or all companies. Dependability is not an absolute, but one individual (Sue) has been with five different companies in 7 years, and may be less dependable than one who has been with 3 companies in 8 years (Patel). Dependability needs to be verified on an interview, as would the reasons for both staying with and leaving a particular company.

From a Culture standpoint, Brian is looking for people who are team players, and who have strong process focus. As he looks across the table all three candidates have had some team leadership roles. Although collaboration will have to be better understood, all three may understand the concept of teamwork. As he looks at the resumés with regard to Process Focus, all candidates have experience with an object-oriented software case tool, which suggests some level of process knowledge.

From a capabilities standpoint, all candidates indicate knowledge of Java and C++. Although we deal with verification of technical competence in Chapter 15, for now take them at their word on technology. So Java and C++ now cease to be discriminators. However, it will be important in the technical interview to probe

Table 13.2 Comparison of Three Candidates to Ideal Hire Profile

| Ideal Hire Profile | Specific Areas | Solutions Architect Position (Highlighted areas indicate potential concerns) | | |
|---|---|---|---|---|
| | | Sue | Patel | Byron |
| Character | Dependability | Five companies in seven years | Three companies in eight years. One involved significant relocation. Took a backward step to upgrade skills | Three companies in eighteen years |
| Culture (Lifestyle and Process) | Collaboration | Team lead | Managed a team of nine people | Team leader and Q/E manager |
| | Process Experience | Rational Rose suggests process focus | PVCS may suggest process focus | Rational Rose suggests process focus |
| Capabilities | Java | Java, Visual Basic, Perl, Python | Java and JavaScript | Java and Java Script |
| | C++ | Yes, plus VC++ | Yes, plus HTML | Yes, plus HTML |
| | Case Tools | Rational Rose, PVCS, Tuxedo, RogueWave Labs | PVCS | Rational Rose |
| Nice to Haves: | XML | Yes | No | Yes |
| | Influence | Descriptive resumé | Management experience | Unknown |

to understand the depth of each candidate's experience with the languages. And both knowledge of and experience with software development tools takes on an increased significance.

"Nice to have" is experience with XML and Influence. Influence is difficult to infer from a resumé, but the way the candidates present their credentials is a reflection of themselves. So, as he looks at the resumés, Brian asks himself about the level of insight each individual has both to their own competencies and to the significance of the role they played on their projects. He looks specifically for instances where individuals were able to recognize the value of the project to the company. Did it impact profitability? Was it a critical project to the company? What was their value to the company?

Now that he has completed his horizontal analysis, he looks vertically at each of the candidates. Wherever an area was either unknown or negative, he has shaded it. He has some concerns about the number of jobs Sue has had; and plans to probe more deeply into that area during the interview process.

- *Develop a list of questions* that will need to be answered to give you clarity about the depth and range of experience each candidate has had. Use each of the areas of experience in the resumé as your guide. Byron has prepared a list of specific questions that he will explore in the interview process. An example of these questions can be found in Table 13.3.

- *Assuming you like this candidate, list the kind of questions you would like to ask of their job references.* Stay focused on what you want to know most. In some instances a consent form signed by the potential employee giving people the right to provide information assists in the process of checking resumés. Some questions you might want to ask a job reference include:

*Would you hire this person back if you could?*
*What are his or her greatest weaknesses and strengths—*
*and how did those qualities show up on the job?*
*If you could design a perfect job for this person, what would it be?*
*Was this person liked by his or her co-workers?*

**Table 13.3** Interview Question Work Sheet

| Candidate | Sue | Byron | Patel |
|---|---|---|---|
| **Dependability** | Why five companies in seven years? It looks as if you change companies every eighteen months. Why? | Why are you looking to leave your current employer? See Chapter 14 for more details | Why are you considering leaving your current employer? See Chapter 14 for more details |
| **Collaboration** | What was the environment at your company? How do the teams work together? How is work distributed? See Chapter 14 | What was the environment at your company? How do the teams work together? How is work distributed? See Chapter 14 | What was the environment at your company? How do the teams work together? How is work distributed? See Chapter 14 |
| **Process Experience** | Tell me about your process for software design | Tell me about your process for software design | Tell me about your process for software design |
| **Software Development Tools** | How have you used Rational Rose? How long have you known it? From whom did you learn it? What experience have you had in implementing solutions using it? | How have you used Rational Rose? How long have you known it? From whom did you learn it? What experience have you had in implementing solutions using it? | How have you used PVCS? How long have you known it? From whom did you learn it? What experience have you had in implementing solutions using it? |

| Software Methodologies | Describe for me your software development methodology. | Describe for me your software development methodology. | Describe for me your software development methodology. |
|---|---|---|---|
| XML | Describe for me how you have used XML. See Chapter 15 for examples of probes for technical depth. | Describe for me how you have used XML. See Chapter 15 for examples of probes for technical depth. | Have you any experience with XML? |
| Influence | This capability can be observed in one underlying theme: How is the candidate handling the rest of the questions? Are they influencing your hiring decision? | This capability can be observed in one underlying theme: How is the candidate handling the rest of the questions? Are they influencing your hiring decision? | This capability can be observed in one underlying theme: How is the candidate handling the rest of the questions? Are they influencing your hiring decision? |

*Look at the companies the person has worked for. What do you know about the cultures of those companies?* Is a person who was happy in that environment likely to be happy in yours? To clarify the culture fit, consider having HR administer the PERForm for Fitability[2] instrument. Also included in Chapter 14 are some questions that you can ask to clarify fit with the culture.

Then map the answers and compare the culture to your own.

- *Rank the resumés* in terms of fit with the Ideal Hire Profile. Things you will want to look for on a resumé:

*Project Responsibilities:* What you want to understand is whether they were at the heart of this project or on the periphery. Who they worked with and the specifics of their role are all important. Also, understanding who they worked for will give you a perspective that is currently lacking.

*Management Responsibilities:* Not all technical people think of supervisory experience as particularly relevant. The candidate may have supervisory ability, but the resumé may not even reflect it. Assuming they supervised others, you may want to ask how the people they supervised differed from one another. This will tell you about how well they perceive differences in others. The number of people they supervised is also relevant, so ask how many they supervised.

*Mentorship or Training experience:* The candidates may have considered an ancillary responsibility of training new employees as unimportant. However, they may have contributed significantly to the growth of the company through growing the people. Ask about this. They may have also acted as an informal mentor to one or more employees. The person who would assume this kind of responsibility is a cut above the rest. The individual who will mentor others is the type of individual who will help to grow your company.

[2]© Irwin & Browning.

*Job Titles:* Many job titles have little meaning outside of the industry, company or department they work for. Job titles are often misleading. Employers sometimes give people titles that obscure the real value of the person. Whether this is done to avoid paying them what they're worth, to make them less attractive to competitors, or because the title has meaning inside of the company is irrelevant.

### Conclusion

It's easy to overlook gold in resumés. Many good people under-market their capabilities. It takes time to go through the resumés and separate the gold from the stones. Unfortunately, there is no easy way to do this.

People who work for smaller companies bring different capabilities to their work. A smaller company is less likely to have a lot of support staff available. Consequently, the person working for a smaller company may have a broader experience set because they have had to rely on their own resources. On the other hand, the level of completeness of a program produced by a small company with a two-week development cycle may not be as robust as that of a larger company with a longer development and QA cycle. It is important to understand exactly the development process of the company, so that you can adequately compare two apparently similar candidates.

# CHAPTER

## 14

# Interview Tactics that Leave No "Wiggle Room"

Evelyn Street walks into your office, meets your eyes with a strong gaze, shakes your hand firmly, but not too firmly, and smiles as she greets you. She is wearing a great-looking outfit, tailored but not stiff, and she carries herself with a poise and assurance that borders on cockiness. You like her instantly. It has taken you about ten seconds to form an impression. And given what you know right now, you'd hire her. How reliable is that information? Unfortunately, not very. But many people make hiring decisions in the first ten seconds of an interview and then use the rest of the time to justify that decision. One in two hires on the average does not meet expectations. So that first information, while providing interesting data, does not tell you anything about how suitable the candidate is for your position. And the cost of a bad hire is several times the annual salary of the employee. Clearly, better methods of choosing people are needed. This chapter illustrates how to sift through a lot of extraneous data and hire the right employees—every time.

Most interviewees are very good at projecting what they think the interviewer is looking for. This chapter proposes a different way of screening prospective employees through some bullet-proof interview tactics that leave no "wiggle room."

Using these tactics requires some planning and practice so that the interview process is comprehensive, courteous, and clear. Remember, perception is going both ways. While you're interviewing the prospective hire, they're interviewing you and comparing you against competing alternatives. The company that is organized and effective says, "We're the right kind of place to work. We make decisions. We have our act together. We're a winner in the marketplace. And, we are serious about you as a candidate." The company that uses outdated interviewing methods, is cumbersome and unclear, also sends a message: "We're not serious about what we're doing." Advance planning is a must.

Good interviewing begins way before the interview—with an "ideal hire" profile discussed in Chapter 11.

We have stated that you will want to select for as few things as possible. In your "ideal hire" profile you will be drawing up a list of desirable qualities, and distinguishing "nice-to-haves" from "must haves." All candidates seriously considered will meet the must-have criteria. Sometimes, when there are a number of candidates to choose from, it is the nice-to-haves that tip the scales toward one candidate or another.

**Your Secret Weapon: Behavioral Interviewing**[1]: The behavioral interview begins like most interviews, by making the interviewee feel comfortable and gaining rapport with the person being interviewed. A good interviewer sets the expectations on the part of the candidate that the interview process may be different from one s/he is used to, but that the goal of the process is to understand as clearly as possible whether or not they would find satisfaction and success in doing the kind of work required of people that will be joining X Co. When conducting a behavioral interview, we tell candidates that they may be interrupted.

---

[1]Behavioral interviewing is based on the pioneering work of Prof. David C. McClelland and Lyle M. Spencer, Ph.D. See the bibliography for more references to their work. Although Spencer used the behavioral interview primarily for employment research, later human resources practitioners applied his work toward selection.

*"I may interrupt you at times, if the information you are providing is not giving me the kind of detail I need. I tell you this now, so that you will not be disconcerted if this happens. Whenever I do this, it is in your best interest. Wasting your time by allowing you to ramble on about a topic that is away from what I am looking for helps neither you nor me."*

If the candidate is experienced, the interviewer usually begins by asking them to tell about their current work and their scope of responsibility. Ask questions to clarify anything you do not understand. You want to be able to distinguish the degree of personal involvement and responsibility in their work. While you are gathering this data, be listening for anything that might be of interest later.

Now the interviewer asks the candidate to recall situations or events in their recent past and tell a story about how they, for example, (a) overcame an obstacle[2] or (b) accomplished something of which they are particularly proud. While the interviewee is recounting the story, the interviewer probes to understand the details.

- **Who** was present? You want to understand not only who was there, but also the roles of the people present.
- **What** were the circumstances? Here you want to understand the specifics of what happened. If they use buzzwords or jargon, ask them to clarify what they mean. In asking for clarification, you are trying to learn their role in the situation. (Were they an observer or the prime mover?)
- **What** events led up to it? You need to understand the history that led up to the event. Understanding the context is really important to your being able to interpret the decisions and actions.
- **When** did it occur? Is this a recent event, or is it ancient history? Ideally, you would like the candidate to go no further back than 18 months. Beyond that, the details of the event get fuzzy, and you are not going to get the behavioral richness of detail that you are looking for.

---

[2]This is an example of a question, but there are many questions—some of which will be covered later in this chapter. The goal of each question is to elicit information that will allow the interviewer to observe specific traits or capabilities.

- **What** was said by **whom**? I frequently ask them to tell me what I would have heard if I were a fly on the wall in the room? What was the tone of voice? Who said what, and what was the chain of dialogue? Often candidates do not volunteer this level of detail unless you press for it, but it can mean all the difference in terms of your level of understanding.
- **What** were they **thinking** at the time? Knowing what was going through the person's mind will give you great insight into their thinking process.
- **How** did they **feel** about what was going on—about the situation and about the other participants? Understanding their feelings gives you insight into whether they were in touch with their feelings and those of others.
- **What** did *they* actually do? In doing so, the interviewer is trying to gain as realistic a picture as possible of the specifics of the event. The reason for clarifying the event is to understand the specific role of the interviewee. Sometimes an interviewee will describe an event by saying, "we all worked together to..." When the interviewer probes more deeply, s/he may find that the actual role of the interviewee was "observer." Or the interviewee may in fact have played a crucial role. Look for soft words: "I've coordinated this or I've recommended that." These words speak to a lack of accountability for results. You will want to understand how accountable the person was for making a real difference. Understanding and clarifying the distinctions of the role specifics means everything in a behavioral interview.

While the interviewee is speaking, the interviewer is either taking copious notes or tape recording the interview. The behavioral interview will follow a similar path, asking about different specific events in the interviewee's past, until the interviewer has gotten sufficient information to make a decision. At the end of the interview, the interviewer asks if the interviewee has any questions, answers the questions, and thanks the interviewee for their time.

In a situation where a company is trying to make a decision about whether or not to hire a particular candidate, the candidate will be given several interviews in succession. In a well-planned interview session, each interviewer will be looking for different information from the candidates.

A rotational schedule will then be set up so that as each candidate rotates from interviewer to interviewer, there is sufficient time for the interviewers between sessions to analyze the information they have received and mentally score the candidate, jotting down any remaining questions that need to be answered on subsequent interviews.

We have included a lot of detail on the Behavioral Interview because its structure is one we recommend you follow when asking a candidate to recall a past event. But the Behavioral Interview is only a part of the process. To paint as complete a picture as possible we recommend that your interview include a number of factors, past behavior being just one of them.

We call this process the Structured Behavioral Interview.

## The Structured Behavioral Interview

- *Life Themes:* Open the interview by having the candidates give a brief history of their lives up until that point. What were the key events that shaped their lives? In reflecting on an individual's past behavior, we suggest you do so with this theme: what has the person done with their time and talent? Also, listen for values. Do they value integrity? How have they demonstrated it? Have they demonstrated courage? What do their stories say about how they feel about hard work? Does their history tell you about how the person feels about diversity? Out of their past, their family, and their environment comes a value for others. Listen for the life themes that shaped their character.

- *Look for passion.* What are they passionate about? Where do their talents lie? When you can combine passion and talent, you have a chance of creating a pretty powerful combination. Have they faced adversity? How has adversity shaped their character? The answers to these questions will tell you a lot about the individual.

**Table 14.1** Interview Plan—Solutions Architect Candidate

| Interviewer | Primary Factor | Secondary Factor |
|---|---|---|
| Brian W. | Integrity | Problem Solving |
| | Dependability | Active Learning |
| | Critical Thinking | |
| Marjorie S. | Technical Breadth | Courage |
| | Sense of Urgency | Collaboration |
| | Integrity | |
| Logan | Experience with Software Design Methodology, and CASE tools such as Rational Rose | Knowledge Transfer |
| | Critical Thinking | Dependability |
| | Collaboration | |

SOURCE: Copyright McGraw-Hill 2001. You may download this worksheet from *www.books. mcgraw-hill.com/training/download*. The document can then be opened, edited, and printed using Microsoft Word or other popular word-processing software.

- *Depth Drills:* Implementing the information provided in Chapters 10 through 12, ask the kind of questions that clarify for you the range and depth of experience—both technical and non-technical—the candidate has presented on the resumé.[3]
- *Critical Events:* Next, ask about two or more critical events that will elicit information on the specific factors that you wish to understand.
- *Simulations:* We also like to balance what they have done in the past with how they will handle unfamiliar situations in the future, so we give the candidates several hypothetical situations and see how they handle them. The combination of past, present, and future is very powerful in analyzing the overall effectiveness of the candidate and in giving you as complete a picture as possible.

Table 14.1 is an interview plan for Brian W. and his colleagues.

Now that each member of the interview team knows what information they are seeking, each will plan questions to trigger this information.

Table 14.2 is Brian W's complete Interview Planning Worksheet.

Majorie's worksheet (Table 14.3) is found on pages 145 and 146. Note the differences in approach, and how the questions complement each other.

**Table 14.2** Interview Planning Worksheet

| Interviewer | Brian W. | Position: | Solutions Architect |
|---|---|---|---|
| Factor | Strategy for Obtaining Information | Question | Notes on Candidate Respons |
| Introduction | Opening Statement | "... My purpose in conducting this interview is to learn about you and to give you a chance to learn about me, my team, and my company, so that we can both make a decision as to whether or not there is a good match between our company and your abilities and goals. <br><br> As the interview progresses, feel free to ask me any questions you have. <br><br> It would help me get to know you better if you would give me a brief history of your career up until this point in time. What are the key events in your life that brought you to this place? | |
| Integrity | Past situation. Looking for issue of integrity and how it was handled. | I'd like you to describe for me the most difficult decision you ever had to make. <br><br> Note: if this question doesn't get you the intended information, ask about a situation where they failed to live up to their own expectations. | |

143

**Table 14.2** Interview Planning Worksheet *(continued)*

| Interviewer | Brian W. | Position: | Solutions Architect |
|---|---|---|---|
| **Factor** | **Strategy for Obtaining Information** | **Question** | **Notes on Candidate Response** |
| Dependability | Situation | *You're in a situation where you have been given two very important assignments that both have a deadline that is not achievable. What do you do?* | |
| Critical Thinking | Looking for past behavior. | *Can you tell me about a particularly challenging customer solution you had to design?* | |
| Problem Solving | Situation | *You've just been called into a customer situation, replacing someone else who left the company. You realize that the solution they had begun to design will not meet the customer's needs without a lot of overhead the design specifications do not call for. What do you do?* | |
| Active Learning<br><br>Look for how they have adapted to the different questions in the interview thus far. You've asked for two instances of past behavior and given them two problem scenarios. By the time they get the second question of the same type, do you see any familiarity with the technique? Jot down your observations. | | | |

SOURCE: Copyright McGraw-Hill 2001. You may download this worksheet from *www.books. mcgraw-hill.com/training/download*. The document can then be opened, edited, and printed using Microsoft Word or other popular word-processing software.

**Table 14.3** Interview Planing Worksheet

| Interviewer | Marjorie S. | Position | Solutions Architect |
|---|---|---|---|
| **Factor** | **Strategy for Obtaining Information** | **Question** | **Notes on Candidate Response** |
| Technical Breadth | Fact Finding | *"(Name), I'd like you to go over your technical history; telling me about your experience with different technologies and projects. I'm specifically interested in what was different about them.* | |
| Sense of Urgency | Looking for past behavior | *Can you describe for me an incident when you were particularly proud of an accomplishment?* | |
| Integrity | Situation | *You have been part of the team that has negotiated the Systems Integration contract with a new client. Your negotiation teams finished in the wee hours of the morning, and everybody (relieved) went home to get a good night's sleep. The client told you they would type up the points agreed to and send them via courier the next morning.* | |
| | | *As you review the points of the agreement, you realize that the client team has made an error—one which is in your favor. You called the person who typed up the agreement and pointed out the error, but he said that that was the agreement. You know this is not the case. What do you do?* | |

**Table 14.3** Interview Planing Worksheet *(continued)*

| Interviewer | Marjorie S. | Position | Solutions Architect |
|---|---|---|---|
| **Factor** | **Strategy for Obtaining Information** | **Question** | **Notes on Candidate Response** |
| Courage | Situation | *You have just replaced an employee who went to a competing firm. She was in the midst of completing the design on a customer solution that has high potential for billable revenue this quarter. Your reputation is on the line to complete the design and get the implementation team working. Without it, your team will not make their goals for this quarter.*<br><br>*As you get closer to the situation, you find that she has overlooked several problems in the design—problems that, if left unsolved, will derail this implementation.*<br><br>*What should you do?* | |
| Collaboration | Past experience | *Tell me about the last project you worked on as part of a team.* | |

**Table 14.4**   Interview Planning Worksheet for Logan

| Interviewer | Logan | Position | Solutions Architect |
|---|---|---|---|
| **Factor** | **Strategy for Obtaining Information** | **Question** | **Notes on Candidate Respons** |
| Experience with Software Design Methodology and CASE tools such as Rational Rose | Fact Finding | *(Name), I'd like you to go over your technical history, telling me about your experience with different CASE tools.*<br><br>*What is the methodology you use when you design a software solution?* | |
| Critical Thinking | Looking for past behavior | *Can you describe for me an incident when you were particularly proud of an accomplishment?* | |
| Collaboration | Situation | *You are a member of a team that has been struggling to finish a very large project on schedule. We have a series of milestone payments that are due at the completion of this project.*<br><br>*One of the members of the project team has become ill, and the team was counting on his participation to meet the schedule.*<br><br>*What would you do?* | |
| Knowledge Transfer | Situation | *A member of your project team has been asking you a lot of questions about your process of software design. She is interested in becoming a solutions architect as well.*<br><br>*She has been asking her manager to sign her up for Rational Rose training, but they will not accept her without a mentor. You are really busy. What would you do?* | |
| Dependability | Past experience | *Can you recall for me a situation where you had a lot at stake for getting a particular job done?* | |

Logan's preparation also takes into account the different areas he is probing for and, where he is looking for a similar capability, uses a different strategy to accomplish it.

Figure 14.5 is a downloadable chart containing sample questions to use in interviewing for different capabilities.

**Table 14.5** Interview Plan—Solutions Architect Candidate

| Capability | Skill | Behavioral Question | Situation |
|---|---|---|---|
| **Character** | | | |
| | Integrity | Can you describe for me a time when you experienced a real ethical dilemma? | You have become aware that a team member whose husband has recently abandoned her has been padding her expense sheet to cover child care. What do you do? |
| | Courage | Can you describe for me a situation where you felt the need to take an unpopular stand because you thought it was the right thing to do? | |
| | Dependability | Can you describe for me a situation where you were in charge and a deadline had to be met?<br><br>Can you recall for me a situation where you had a lot at stake for getting a particular job done? | It's Friday afternoon at 4:30 p.m., and Joe, a client, has left a message on your voice-mail that a solution your team is contracted to develop is giving intermittent errors and dropping data. The client wants you to work over the weekend to help isolate the issues before they go live on Monday.<br><br>Saturday is your daughter's third birthday. What do you do? |

| Capability | Skill | Behavioral Question | Situation |
|---|---|---|---|
| | Trustworthiness | | You are the chief programmer on the DIR code. The deal calls for stiff penalties for missed deadlines. There is a requirement that the program be able to send and receive updated information via the Internet. You have just learned that a small error has been found in one of the operating modules that will cause errors in data transmission. The team has informed you that the error will affect quarter-end processing, and will not be a factor for six weeks. They assure you that the error should be repaired before then. What do you do? |
| Learning | Active Learning | NOTE: Active learning can be assessed via instruments such as the Watson-Glaser. In addition, observation of how the interviewees learn from the beginning to the end of the interview process will give you good data. | Simulations can be used to assess Active Learning. Generally, they will be longer and more involved than time permits including in an interview. |

**Table 14.5** Interview Plan—Solutions Architect Candidate *(Continued)*

| Capability | Skill | Behavioral Question | Situation |
|---|---|---|---|
| | Knowledge Transfer | | A member of your project team has been asking you a lot of questions about your process of software design. She is interested in becoming a solutions architect as well.<br><br>She has been asking her manager to sign her up for Rational Rose training, but they will not accept her without a mentor. You are really busy. What would you do? |
| | Developing Others | Can you describe a situation where you acted as a coach to others? | Paul, the software specialist on your project, has become erratic lately, and deadline slips are frequent. You understand that he has requested time away from the office to work on his part alone. You suspect that there may be an issue of technical ability. What do you do? |
| Analyzing | | | |
| | Technical Depth | | Ask participant to code a particular solution on a white board. Leave the room, and give him 20 minutes. |

| Capability | Skill | Behavioral Question | Situation |
|---|---|---|---|
| | Technical Breadth | Can you describe the most recent project that you worked on? What was your role? What specifically did you do? Who else was involved? | Use a team approach and question the candidate about his or her ability to solve a series of technical problems in all areas where he claims expertise. |
| | Business Acumen | Can you describe for me a situation that tested your business knowledge? | You have been brought in to trouble shoot a problem the customer has been having with its recent company-wide Linux implementation. You believe a technically superior solution might involve scrapping Linux and going to Windows NT. What do you do? |
| | Problem Solving | Can you describe for me a particularly thorny problem that you were pleased to solve? | |
| | Decisiveness | Can you describe for me a situation when you had to quickly make a decision? | |
| Relating | | | |
| | Perceptiveness | NOTE: Perceptiveness can be observed in how the interviewee responds to the different styles of the interviewers. Do they show sensitivity for the task you are trying to accomplish? Do they "connect" with you? | Your manager was openly critical of your work in a team meeting. You were embarrassed in front of your peers. What do you do? |

**Table 14.5** Interview Plan—Solutions Architect Candidate *(Continued)*

| Capability | Skill | Behavioral Question | Situation |
|---|---|---|---|
| | Influence | Can you describe for me a situation where you had to sway the opinions of others? | NOTE: Influence can be observed situationally in how well the interviewee handles being interviewed. Are they able to influence you to want to hire them? Are they clear and forceful in their communication? Is their body language attentive? |
| | Collaboration | Can you recall a situation where you had to work with others to accomplish something? | You are a member of a team that has been struggling to finish a very large project on schedule. You have a series of milestone payments that are due from the customer at the completion of this project. One of the members of the project team has become ill, and the team was counting on his participation to meet the schedule. What would you do? |
| | Customer Insight | Can you recall for me a particularly difficult customer situation? | |

| Capability | Skill | Behavioral Question | Situation |
|---|---|---|---|
| Performing | | | |
| | Sense of Urgency | Can you recall for me a time when you were really on the hook to make something happen? | |
| | Execution | Can you describe a time when the whole team had to pull together to make something happen? | |
| | Drive to Achieve | Can you describe how you approach meeting goals and commitments? Can you describe a time when you missed a goal? | You are a new project manager in the IT department. Your biggest internal customer has come to you with a problem and wants you to drop everything to help them implement it quickly. What do you do? |
| | Accomplishment | Can you describe for me some accomplishments you are particularly proud of? How is your performance measured today? What has been your performance against your goals? | |
| | Optimism | Can you describe a time when everything seemed to go wrong? | |

# Conducting the Technical Part of the Interview

In Chapter 14 we described how to do a Structured Behavioral Interview. This chapter expands on the topic of the interview, and focuses on the question, "How can you tell whether the individual is qualified technically?" Like the interviews in Chapter 14, the technical "depth drill" is a structured behavioral interview. However, its sole focus is to qualify technical competence.

You have three technical candidates, and they all look great on paper, but the question is "How can I know before they walk in the door that they have got what it takes technically?" In researching this chapter we talked to a number of people who have reputations for conducting a good technical interview. We were trying to learn their secrets, so that we could pass them along to you, but more importantly, we were attempting to discern any principles that applied to all situations.

As we planned this chapter, we realized that the easy thing would be to say "Just have your technical person really grill them." This is, in fact, the best piece of advice we can give you, but you've probably thought of that yourself. So we looked at the problem from the following perspectives:

- What is it that's unique about technical ability? How can one identify raw talent?
- And secondly, we wondered whether there were any principles that applied to evaluating technical knowledge.

### What is unique about the techie?

When we profiled all of the technical roles using the capabilities model presented in Chapter 11, we noticed that all of them were stronger in the Analyzing capability and in Active Learning. As you may recall, the Analyzing Capability measures the breadth and depth of a person's technical knowledge, their ability to think critically, solve problems rapidly, and make sound business decisions. The person who is good technically tends to be stronger in critical thinking, tends to approach problems from a logical perspective. He or she can listen to something described, mentally order the process in a very linear fashion, break it down into logical chunks, turn those logical chunks into business functions. To test for critical thinking:

- Pose a problem to the candidate. It may be in their area of technical expertise, or it may not. What you want to look for is how their mind approaches the process of understanding the problem. If you pose a problem to a budding Sherlock, you should be getting a lot of questions, and the questioning process should be looking at the problem from all perspectives. If you get a snap answer, either the candidate is not good at critical thinking, or you haven't really tested their critical thinking ability. To understand which of the two alternatives is true, you pose a more difficult problem—perhaps one with which the candidate has no familiarity—and observe how they approach it.
- Have your HR department administer *The Watson-Glaser Critical Thinking Appraisal.* This is a reading comprehension test that measures the candidate's ability to think conceptually, recognize assumptions, deduce, interpret and evalu-

ate arguments. The Watson-Glaser also tests whether the candidate's ability to reason is affected by emotion.

Critical thinking will sustain you when the answers aren't obvious. The person who has confidence in their ability to think critically is not intimidated by the unknown. In an industry where last year's technology is already outdated, it is the critical thinker who will push forward the frontiers of knowledge. Business Acumen and Decision Making have at their core Problem Solving and Critical Thinking, but knowledge of how a business operates and how a particular problem affects not only the company but also the client base comes with experience.

The capability that fuels the development of the techie is Active Learning. By active learning we mean the pure thirst for knowledge. The scientist who has chosen technology as his or her field is both highly intelligent and intellectually curious. They are sitting out there on the bleeding edge of a technology that re-invents itself every six months. So, the people that will be most successful in this field are those whose drive to learn is internally fueled. Although they described it differently, all of the companies we interviewed both identified and valued this capability.

Kelly New, Chief Technology Officer of ecIndx, a supply chain optimization company in the e-commerce arena, looks for people who are intellectually aggressive. He wants people who just can't stand not knowing about something, people who are real tech junkies, who know all the nooks and crannies on the Internet where information can be found.

Bennie Slone, Director of the MidSouth Area for Compaq's Professional Services group, looks for people whose background demonstrates that they have done a lot of self-learning. With the pace of change as fast as it is, he knows he cannot afford to train them on everything. So he looks for people self-motivated enough to learn on their own.

Things that tell you whether the person is an active learner...

- The Active Learner has typically been involved in a lot of extracurricular activity. This activity may be technology-related, or it may not. Ask about their hobbies and clubs they belong to.

- The Active Learner is an information digest. Ask about what they like to read. What business and professional journals do they subscribe to? What books are they now reading? What was the most interesting book they've read in the last year?
- The *Weschler Adult Intelligence Survey* (WAIS) is a classic intelligence test that asks test takers to organize data into meaningful patterns or sequences.

To understand what the candidate has learned from experience:

- Apply the techniques learned in Chapter 14 Structured Behavioral Interview and explore in depth recent project assignments. Some questions that might help you explore the depth of project experience are:

*What was the purpose of the project?*
*What was your role in the project?*
*Who else worked on the project?*
*What specifically did you do?*
*Why did you approach the project in the way you did?*
*What influenced your choice?*
*What problems did you encounter?*
*What would you do differently?*
*What did you learn from the experience?*
*What would the customer say about the project?*
*How did the project impact the company?*
*Were there any project team members that
you would rather not work with again?*
*Why?*
*Would you do another project with this customer?*
*Why?*

As the candidate reveals more information about the project, there will be opportunities for your technical people with equivalent or better knowledge to do "depth drills" on technology approaches. A general principle to apply is to keep getting more specific until you understand exactly what the individual did and knows, and where the limits of their knowledge lie.

### Evaluating technical knowledge—the "depth drill"

The "depth drill" must be done by another technical person of equivalent or superior ability. Don't try to do this yourself, unless you have experience equal or superior to the candidate. As hiring manager, you should inform the technical interviewer of the areas of technical expertise that are most important to you, so that they can probe more deeply in those areas.

Although each of our expert technical interviewers approached the interviews differently, some principles could be inferred.

- Talent attracts talent. Use the "depth drill" as an opportunity to showcase your in-house technical talent. Your goal here should be to make sure that the applicant feels challenged. Chris Rouland of ISS uses a team approach. Because he recruits from all over the country, he does an initial telephone screen, using two or three technologists of superior skill to the skills claimed on the resumé. Their goal is to take the individual to the absolute limit of his or her knowledge. Most applicants are expeected to fail this technical interview. It is not an absolute disqualifier, as long as the interviewee has demonstrated the level of proficiency they are looking for. If the applicant doesn't fail this interview, Rouland gets very aggressive in recruiting them. This is actually a very smart approach. Good technology people want to feel challenged[1]. The depth of the interview will actually sell the candidate on working for your company.
- Go from general to specific. Keep asking for more detail until you understand exactly what they did and what they know. An example of a tech drill might go as follows:

[1]I am reminded of when my son arrived at Massachusetts General Hospital to begin a fellowship in Clinical Neurophysiology. His first day on the job he was asked to present a problem before a group of fellow physicians, and they took him to the limits of his knowledge. Once he got over the feeling of wondering whether he had measured up, he was invigorated by what he would learn during the fellowship.

*"...I wrote a servlet in JAVA.[2]"*

**"What platform did you write it on?"**

*"UNIX"*

**"What did it interface with?
Did it pull anything from the database?"**

*"Yeah, actually it pulled data from Oracle. It pulled these three tables."*

**"Then what did it do with the tables once it got it?"**

*"Oh, actually I had to write this parcer which went through
and it pulled out the address, and then it had to then change
the address to this format and present it on a web page."*

**"Oh really, how did you present it?
What did the applet use to interface with the browser?"**

*"Actually, I had to generate ASP on the fly..."*

- Challenge their assumptions. There are five or ten legitimate ways to solve every technical problem. Ask them why they chose a particular approach, and make them defend it.
- Make them prove it. ISS and Lehman Brothers will ask an applicant to code something that they claim to know on a white board, leave them alone for twenty minutes, and come back and see what they've done.
- Validate their skill through others. Dr. Anindya Datta, CEO of ChutneySystems and a former professor of Computer Science at Georgia Tech, does a multi-level reference check on senior technical people. He talks to a peer, the manager of the person, and a subordinate.
- Understand the development culture they support. Datta wants to understand whether they come from an environment that supports a long or short development cycle. Those who come from a mature company may be used to long development cycles where a slippage of two months on a development schedule does not mean much. In an emerging company, a slippage of two months on a development cycle

---

[2] Thanks to Ross Rankin, Chief Technology Officer of MediaOcean, for this mini depth drill.

could mean a loss of funding. In addition, the shorter development cycle has more stress built into it, so the person's ability to work under stress is a significant consideration.

• Give them a current problem.[3] If you are struggling with a problem and haven't figured out how to attack it, pose it to the candidate and see what they can do with it. You may get an additional insight into the problem while you gain insight into the candidate's thinking process.

## Conclusion

As you can see, there are many different styles of qualifying technical talent. The important thing to remember about it is to look at the whole job the person needs to be able to do, and drill deeply in the areas critical to you. But solutions to technical problems are as often people problems as they are technical, so don't focus solely on technology. Understand how the individual will fit into your work culture.

[3]Thanks to Kipp Jones, Vice President of Internet Technologies at VideoNetworks for this idea.

# Keeping Winners

## CHAPTER

# 16

# Creative Compensation Strategies

IF YOU HOPE this chapter holds a magic formula for hiring better people for less money, forget it. Good IT talent isn't cheap. (For that matter, neither is mediocre IT talent.) Tech-savvy employees earn 78 percent more than workers do generally, and the gap is just getting wider.

Let's face it: people are in short supply. Employees are in a very strong position when it comes to money, and that's not likely to change anytime soon.

This *doesn't* mean that the almighty dollar is the be-all and end-all for technology professionals. It simply means that as an employer your cost of entry is steeper now than it's ever been. Once you accept that, you'll discover ways to put together compensation packages that motivate, reward and retain good workers while weeding out the rest.

Step one in developing a good compensation strategy is to compare your pay package to what the rest of the world has to offer. Don't make assumptions here, and don't unquestioningly accept your finance department's view of the situation ("Look, we just gave everybody a $2500 raise. They've got absolutely nothing to complain about.")

One good way to find out how your pay policy measures up is to come right out and ask. Here's how.

*Conduct exit interviews.* Ask departing employees what they think of their pay and benefits. Urge them to quantify their opinions. ("On a scale of one to five, with five being outstanding, how do you rate your compensation here at Bigbucks Inc.?") Tracking down workers 90 days after departure for post-exit interviews is also helpful, because it uncovers information obvious only in hindsight. A younger staffer, for example, may not be experienced enough to accurately judge what you were paying until he or she has worked somewhere else for a few months.

*Conduct anonymous employee surveys.* Two cautions: the wording of these surveys is important, and privacy for the respondents is essential. This is nothing to stumble into unprepared, so have the work designed and administered by an HR professional.

*Meet with employees one-on-one.* These meetings can be real eye-openers. You might discover that Joe would rather have a four-day week than another $10K, Suzie will stay put for another year if she can telecommute three days a month, and those guys who bailed out of the networking group did so because their manager's a jerk, not because they were dissatisfied with their salaries.

This last point is important. Many employees cite salary as a primary reason for leaving, although in fact there may be something else to blame. The first 90 days on a new job are critical, and if certain things happen—or don't happen—during that period, the employee's likely to leave no matter what you're paying. At risk are new employees who (1) don't understand what's expected of them, (2) get caught in the political machinery, (3) don't receive direct support and feedback from their boss (or don't like their boss) (4) aren't trained properly, or (5) are never made to feel welcome.

The quickest way to find out what's important to people is to ask them. You may be pleasantly surprised at how easily you can give them what they want. It's usually far easier, and less expensive, to accommodate good workers than to replace them.

If you need convincing on the last point, here are a couple of interesting statistics. The Corporate Leadership Council estimates that the direct cost of hiring a new associate is 15 to 30 percent of salary, with a typical position taking about 45 days to fill. The indirect cost—lost productivity and so forth—is as high as 70 to 85 percent. But here's the kicker: if you bring in the wrong person, that's just chickenfeed.

*Augment employee feedback with industry salary surveys.* The Internet abounds with salary information, but don't forget that timeliness and specificity are everything. Surveys more than a year old are useless, and so is data that doesn't reflect your company's size, geographic location and type of business. Check *www.jobstar.org* for links to several hundred salary surveys. Other resources include the Bureau of Labor Statistics (*www.bls.gov*), and the Economic Research Institute (*www.erieri.com*).

PriceWaterhouseCoopers, KPMG, and the American Electronics Association publish in-depth reports every year with compensation data sliced and diced from every angle, and trade publications are another useful resource for salary and benefit information.

*Third-party consultants can be invaluable.* When a consultant says your company's paying peanuts, it's a little easier to take than when an employee (departing for a five-figure raise) says the same thing. A good consultant can usually recommend compensation repairs that are often less drastic, and less expensive to implement, than anything your management team would come up with on its own.

Now that you know where your company's compensation stands vis à vis the competition, you can rectify pay inequities according to a master plan. Simply raising salaries doesn't work, because it fuels wage inflation and creates a sense of entitlement. (In the words of a software entrepreneur who learned the hard way, "You can never pay enough to people who have an over-inflated value of themselves.")

The next step is to remind your employees exactly what they *are* getting. If your company hasn't compiled a one-page list of every perk, benefit and bonus opportunity it offers—right down to the Starbucks in the break room and free parking—you're missing a key recruiting and retention tool. Don't wait for the folks in marketing to come up with a six-color brochure. Type out a single-spaced, bulleted list and run it by two or three other people to catch anything you may have left out. Let the window sticker on a new car be your guide: no feature is unimportant, including the four-way flashers and the rear-view mirror. Once this list is complete you'll undoubtedly be astonished at how rich, comprehensive, and competitive your comp package already is. Most important, you've armed yourself and your employees with an at-at-glance laundry list that competing employers must meet or beat. Odds are they haven't compiled one of their own, so you're already ahead.

Now for step three: developing compensation packages that reflect the needs and wants of the *individuals* on your payroll. Here are a few ideas to spark your thinking.

*Share the pie.* If you have the authority to offer equity and haven't done so, why not? More and more employees understand, and expect, the responsibilities of ownership and are willing to work hard to earn it. There are hundreds of ways to structure employee ownership that can protect your firm, motivate workers, preserve management control, and minimize the tax hit.

These range from the sublime to the ridiculous, with *Business Week* reporting an example of the latter: some Internet companies are reportedly giving recruits half their salaries as low-interest loans, thereby reducing income taxes for the employee and payroll costs for the employer. Workers repay their loans only if the stock jumps by a certain percent. (The bad news for everybody, of course, is that of the roughly 80 companies that went public during the first quarter of 2000, almost half are now trading below their IPO price—and 90 percent are trading below their day one close.)

At the other end of the spectrum is an ingenious approach CEO Naveen Jain takes to give employees a piece of the action at Redmond, WA-based InfoSpace. Jain has created a $30 million fund so his employees can actually become part-time venture capitalists. All 500 employees are eligible to invest, but must stay at the company three years to cash out. (This investment opportunity is over and above the employee stock option plan.)

If you don't have the personal authority to put an equity-sharing plan in place, don't worry about it. But accept the fact that you must make the effort to create an environment where individual contributions are recognized and handsomely rewarded.

*Pay for performance.* In May 2000, consulting firm Towers Perrin released the results of an international study that indicates top-performing companies—those whose shareholder returns are consistently in the top quartile—don't reward employees the same way middle-of-the-pack firms do.

Four differences stand out. First, the most successful companies consistently pay top performers more than other employees, including bigger base pay increases, higher variable pay awards, and so on. Second, paying for performance is the *basis* of their compensation strategy, not an afterthought. Third, they realize—and act upon—the fact that today's employees want different things from employers than prior generations did. Finally, they communicate *often* and *openly* about the financial rewards that strong individual contributors receive.

Corporate America hates to talk about money with employees, but the companies that really make pay-for-performance work seem to have gotten over that. According to Towers Perrin, they spend significantly more time, money and effort making sure their employees understand the key aspects of how their pay is determined. They use the Web and e-mail more intensely for internal communications, and they're *twice* as likely to measure the success of those communications.

Paying for performance is a sure-fire way to distinguish the A and B players from the Cs—*as long as you send consistent messages to underperformers* via reduced pay, constructive feedback, and mentoring.

It's worthwhile to get the incentive-based pay thing right, because this phenomenon isn't going away. At least one consulting firm predicts that within the next year or so, variable compensation will account for 10 percent of the total wages paid in the United States.

*Rethink your benefits package.* DaimlerChrysler AG has added a work/family account to its benefits package, giving professional, administrative and managerial workers $8000 to use for child care, elder care, adoption assistance, retirement—whatever they see fit.

If your employees are primarily young, healthy workers who don't see the value of heavy-duty health insurance, long-term disability coverage and traditional retirement plans, why offer them? Ditto for speculative, high-risk/reward benefits that don't appeal to more seasoned employees. Cookie-cutter benefits packages squander money and valuable recruiting opportunities.

Next time you conduct a salary survey, ask your employees about their benefits preferences. You might discover they would willingly trade that bells-and-whistles PPO for no-frills health coverage if it means they can now have a beefed-up training allowance and a subsidized PC purchase plan.

Speaking of PCs, remember when Delta Airlines, Ford Motor Company and Intel announced free personal computers for all employees? The idea works for virtually any organization, even those that aren't Fortune 50 behemoths. A 35-person software firm introduced a computer purchase program in 1999 with extraordinary results. All but one person participated, and the peripheral benefits—great goodwill among spouses and kids and a positive impact on retention—are gravy. The company reimburses 50 percent of any hardware or software purchased for home use, up to $1800 per 24-month period. ("Not one person who took advantage of the PC purchase program voluntarily left the company," the president says.)

*The opportunity to learn is priceless.* In fact, it's a key motivator for technology professionals. Steve McConnell, author of *Rapid Development: Taming Wild Software Schedules*, says that the top three motivators for programmer analysts are achievement, possibility for growth, and the work itself. Despite this, employers are often reluctant to make the most of their tech workers' hunger to learn. *Why should I pay for Susan's MCSE accreditation? She'll just use it to leverage a better job somewhere else.*

The odds are that Susan will leave your company whether you pay for her MCSE accreditation or not. But if you *don't* provide ongoing education she'll probably leave even sooner. Smart employers also see training as integral to their compensation structure. They position it exactly that way to potential employees and protect it fiercely from the bean counters.

Home Depot, named by ComputerWorld in 2000 as the best place to work for IT professionals, invests a whopping $9000 in training per person every year, and employees devote about 17 days annually to ongoing education. Home Depot's IT turnover is 3 percent, with 98 percent of its people on staff for five years or more. Avon Products keeps turnover to 8 percent and spends $10,000 a year on training. (Industry-wide the IT churn rate hovers between 20 and 30 percent, with certain parts of the country topping 50 percent.)

Educational support can be as sweeping as sponsoring an accelerated master's degree program through a local University (an employee benefit offered by Federal Express) or as basic as a bonus for those who complete technical certification course. More and more companies are allowing employees to learn during work hours. Even the smallest firms are finding that when they provide on-the-job training, study time and lab time, the employee provides the effort.

*Time is money—literally.* Many IT executives say flexible hours and telecommuting are two of their most effective low-cost incentives. If your company doesn't have flextime and telecommuting policies in place, why not? And if you *do* offer them, but your corporate culture frowns on employees who actually use them, go back and re-read Chapter 4. It's hard to keep superstars (or anyone else) if you promise one thing and reward something very different.

The creative possibilities for flextime are endless. Sabbaticals are now coming into vogue, and some firms offer up to six months off with pay for every three years worked. San Rafael, CA-based Autodesk Inc. offers six-week sabbaticals every four years and doesn't limit the number of days employees take for personal or sick leave. (Autodesk workers also set their own hours.) Before you reach for the smelling salts, hear what Dexter Senft of Lehman Brothers has to say.

"Paying an employee to take six months off every three years is only a 16 percent premium," he says. "For the individual who just wants to go off mountain climbing, or to spend six months with the family, it's a great proposition."

Any compensation strategy that helps employees bring their personal and work lives into equilibrium gives you a hiring and retention edge. In a 1999 PriceWaterhouseCoopers survey of 2500 college students in 11 countries, 57% percent said that work/life balance is their primary career goal. Four-day workweeks, staggered shifts, longer work days with every tenth day off...they're all variations on the theme.

*Turn relocation packages into a recruiting, retention and compensation tool.* If you're hiring people outside your local market, the quality of your relocation package influences both whether your offer will be accepted *and* how the employee's family feels about the new company. Moving is traumatic, and family resistance is the number one deal-killer for corporate transfers. If you're going after high-demand talent, your relocation package had better be pretty exceptional.

Corporate relocation expenses in all industries have gone up nearly 27 percent since 1990. You'll be expected to offer least one preview trip to the new community for the employee and spouse in addition to paying the traditional relocation expenses—moving, temporary housing, real estate closing costs and attorneys fees. *Time* magazine reports that some employers who bring people into areas with a higher cost of living actually provide monthly mortgage subsidies for the first three to five years.

Subsidized housing for non-homeowners, in fact, may be an idea whose time has come. Forty percent of households in Santa Clara, CA can't afford the rent on a two-bedroom apartment, while 65,000 families in the same city have a net worth of over $1 million—*not* counting their home value. If your employee population is primarily young and single (and even if it isn't), take a tip from West Coast ski areas, which subsidize housing for their resort staff during the season. (Nobody but tourists can afford the accommodations at most ski areas.)

*Don't forget the stuff money can't buy.* All the money in the world won't lower your churn rate if your people don't feel challenged or appreciated. "If you work for Attila the Hun, somebody handing you a check for $50 is like rubbing salt in a wound," says one disgruntled programmer analyst. "If I can go down the street for an immediate $10,000 salary bump, you need to be giving out more than $10,000 worth of 'good feelings'. Not sloppy gushing, but praise and mentoring."

# CHAPTER 17

# Five Steps Out the Door: Tactics to Avoid Unwanted Turnover

Scenario 1: You are in charge of application development in an internal IT department of a large corporation. You are ready to begin a major, high visibility project for one of your most important customers. You have spent weeks putting together the team to complete the job. You have introduced them to your customers. In fact, it was the reputation of one of the team members that led the customer to decide to do the work in-house and retain IT to complete it. Your key employee has just completed his fact-finding, and is ready to go to preliminary design. Your reputation is on the line, because you sold this project to your management, who in turn gave it high visibility with theirs. Everything is going great until your key employee resigns at the end of the workday. When you review the fact-finding notes taken in preparation to begin preliminary design, you find that they are scant and unintelligible...

Scenario 2: You are one year into implementation of a large systems integration project for a major client. You are coming to a point of collection of payment for several major milestones that are nearing completion. You have forecasted the revenue to your manager, and she in turn has forecasted it to hers. The project is expected to continue for at least three more years, and represents a substantial portion of your performance quota. All aspects of the project are going well, and you anticipate no problems. That is, until your Program Manager walks in and resigns to go to a competitor. Shortly thereafter you learn that the competitor is offering to take over the project...

**Scenario 3:** You are in charge of product development for a high tech startup. You are an internet infrastructure company and are in your first round of venture capital financing. You are developing product to tight windows, and a delay in product launch would signal concern to your financial partners. Product development is right on schedule until your chief architect leaves suddenly. The VC wants to meet with you immediately...

Although all three scenarios are presented as "blind sides," in fact, employees don't just decide to leave your company overnight. What may appear as a sudden decision to you has actually been brewing for perhaps months. In spite of what you might hear in an exit interview, most people do not arbitrarily leave a place where they are happy. Anyone who has told you that is being less than truthful with you. They may have been recruited away, or they may have left voluntarily. However, most do not leave on a whim. At any point in time approximately 40 percent[1] of your workers are considering leaving your company. This chapter explores some of the "Early Warnings" that might provide you insight into a potential defection prior to having lost a valuable employee.

The good recruiters are out there. They are making a lot of money moving people from company to company. And daily they are establishing relationships with your people, cataloging their wants, and looking for opportunities to place them else-

[1] This figure is based upon the research done by the authors. We surveyed 3000 tech workers, and tabulated responses from 362 workers.

where. Your employee's dialogue with a potential recruiter might go something like this:

- **Bullet Proof:** *"I'm completely happy with my employer. Don't bother me or waste my time talking to me about other opportunities."* This employee is not considering leaving. They are completely satisfied with your company, with their vision of themselves as part of your company, and are not vulnerable to competitive inroads. This is the bucket where you want all of your key employees to fall.
- **Not Looking:** *"I'm pretty happy with my current employer. You can tell me about what you've got, but you're probably wasting my time and yours."* This is the typical employee. They are not really shopping around, but they have one vulnerability factor and can be talked into listening to what's available on the market. And that's only a step away from Early Warning. Depending on the marketability of the employee, "Not Looking" can quickly become "History." Proactivity is the secret to resolving vulnerability.
- **Early Warning:** *"Overall, I'm pretty satisfied with where I am right now, but I'd like to hear about what's out there."* If you're like most companies out there, this bucket represents the widest section of the bell curve. Overall the employee is pretty satisfied with their current situation, but two or more vulnerability factors are keeping them from being immune to competitive pressure.
- **Vulnerable:** *"Actually, I've begun thinking about looking around. I'm a little less than satisfied with . . . "* This employee is probably showing more than two vulnerability indicators, and the level of intensity is somewhat high. With prompt attention to fixing the problems, this employee can still be turned around. However, it is more difficult to ward off a competitive threat once dialogue has begun with other companies.
- **History:** *"I'm glad you called. I was just getting around to calling you."* This employee is most likely beyond saving. They have begun to actively dialogue with other companies. Once

the employee mentally crosses over and becomes a "candidate," it is very difficult to turn the situation around. It is never impossible, but the farther down the path the employee advances, the more committed they become to another company.

### Vulnerability Factors—Early Warnings

"Red sky at morning, sailor's warning." Just like the aphorism, there are certain factors that can give insights into potential vulnerabilities. We have grouped them into four categories:

- Challenge
- Change
- Leadership
- Compensation

### Challenge

Our research indicates that the biggest reason people join a company has to do with the opportunity for personal growth. Techies are learning engines. They want to be challenged on a daily basis. Once the job ceases to provide opportunities for growth, you stand to lose them. So here's the rub. Just about the time that they get really good at what they are doing, they also stop learning and want to do something else. Technologists see a direct correlation between learning the latest technology and their value in the talent marketplace. Things that can affect the level of challenge in work are:

- **Your biggest client wants to extend your most talented consultant** beyond the end of the engagement. You can bill out the consultant to support the transfer of the solution to the client; however, the new learning to the consultant is in the 10 percent range. A project or engagement is an implied contract between you and the people who work on them. Projects—or engagements—have a beginning and an end. There is an expectation that the engagement will end within a specified period of time. Agreement to extend a consultant might be seen as a betrayal. If a client wants to extend the engagement, look for an opportunity to transition another consultant for whom the work would be a challenge into the engagement and reassign the experienced consultant to an engagement that will be interesting. Allow the experienced consultant to mentor the consultant that is being transitioned into the engagement.

- Jean has been **in the same job for six years now.** She doesn't complain, but you notice that she has become quiet lately... Evaluate the work your people are doing. Look for opportunities to provide enrichment. It doesn't have to be a new job. Perhaps a task force assignment, a new project, or some training might provide the needed challenge.

- Stephen's **mentor has just left the company.** This creates both a relationship and a development void. Quickly find another mentor, and evaluate whether or not training on a new technology or methodology might be in order.

- **Development is spotty and unplanned.** Put together a development plan that meets both the business' needs and those of your people. Suffice it to say that leaving development to chance is ignoring one of your most powerful weapons in fighting lack of challenge.

### Change

Change creates uncertainty, and people are uneasy with uncertainty. They want to take action to reassert control over events that have overtaken them. This climate of uncertainty can propel an employee to look outside of your company for the stability they seek. The kinds of factors that can create a sense of uncertainty and loss of control are:

- **The Culture of the Company Changes.** The kind of things that affect the culture of the company are certain precipitating events, such as...

  o The company is sold
  o The company is merged with another

- The company acquires another company
- Restructuring or downsizing
- Reorganizations
- Competitive pressure
- Performance pressure
- New leadership
- Growth and maturation of the enterprise

If the culture changes, talk about it. Give employees an opportunity to voice their concerns, desires, and preferences. Sometimes recognition of the change is sufficient for employees to come to grips with it.

- **Employee Transition.** Perhaps a project or assignment is coming to an end. Perhaps a sponsor leaves the company or is demoted. For whatever reason, the employee perceives that his or her situation in the company is at some level of risk. Understanding when an employee is going through a transition and communicating with them about their value to the company can make all the difference. Don't wait for the employee to bring it up. Be proactive in addressing the issue.
- **Changes at Home.** A spouse is relocated. An employee marries, divorces, experiences death of a family member, has a child... All signal life changing events that can upset employee equilibrium. Sensitivity to the changes that an employee is experiencing can help to offset them. If someone who works for you is going through a divorce, you may have to temporarily ease up some of the pressure of the work environment. The employee who has been up all night with a newborn may need some relief. Perhaps you can give the new father a day off to assist with a sick child. Perhaps you can ease the workload temporarily on an employee who is under stress. The key to dealing effectively with change is good communication and sensitivity to the needs of others. Keep the channels of communication open. Talk with the employee about what's happening. Ask how you can help. Let the event be an opportunity to build loyalty.

## Leadership

Leadership is one of the most important factors affecting employee turnover. If an employee has a negative perception of his/her manager, he or she is are more likely to leave. In addition, conflicts of philosophy, approach, values, or work ethic between the employee and the manager may precipitate turnover. Chapter 19 deals with the role of leadership in employee retention.

## Compensation

Research has consistently rated compensation as fourth or fifth in the list of retention motivators, but that doesn't mean it isn't important. Employees may not be totally motivated by money, but they do seek equitable compensation. Our experience is that compensation is a factor that becomes important when one or more of the other factors are also present. It's as if it is a multiplying factor. The importance of money as a motivator varies from person to person and culture to culture. In the results-based culture, compensation tends to be more important, because it is used to offset other sacrifices the employee must make to provide the sought-after results. Compensation issues can be either real or perceived. If the employee perceives that there is a compensation inequity, they feel betrayed.

If an employee has been trained on a particularly exciting technology or methodology, his or her value in the marketplace has increased. Recruiters like to target graduates of training programs because they know that there is a lag between when the employee is trained and his or her compensation reflects his or her increased value in the marketplace. Be proactive in fixing pay equity issues, and above all talk about it with your employee.

## Red Flags

Employees do not necessarily tell you that they are considering leaving. Not, that is, in so many words. However, their behavior may speak volumes. If any of the following Red Flags are present, you should increase your expectation that if things do not change immediately, the employee will probably leave:

- **Loss of Intensity.** When an employee makes a mental decision to leave, they disengage. Subtle clues might be that a person who was intensely focused on the business is now less so. It might manifest itself by leaving on time, instead of one hour late each day. Or, the person might not take that customer call five minutes before closing time.
- **Withdrawing from Others.** When an employee makes a mental decision to defect, they begin the process of "leaving" the people they work with. The level of enthusiasm they bring to work diminishes, so they have less in common with those who are excited about what they do. They stop being involved with others. Perhaps they are busy when the group goes to lunch, or when team meetings occur.
- **Conflict with Others.** Some people begin saying "goodbye" by saying to themselves, "I didn't really like that person, anyway."
- **Rumor Mill Says They are "Looking" or "Leaving."** The rumor mill is right better than 90 percent of the time. So if you are hearing it on the rumor mill, believe it and take action.
- **Change in Behavior.** The normally talkative person becomes quiet. The mild mannered person develops a short fuse. The normally fastidious person begins leaving things undone. Any change in behavior is a signal that something is wrong. Don't ignore it.
- **Employee Initiates Compensation Discussion.** Although compensation may be the precipitating factor, this employee is attempting to understand his or her value to you. Compensation is a less emotional way of talking about it. They may have felt "passed over" for a key assignment; they may have seen others rewarded in ways that suggest inequity. Do not ignore this signal. Ask the employee to share their feelings with you. Look at the issue from his or her perspective. If there is an inequity, do something to correct it.

As part of your management process, consider implementing the Vulnerability Assessment tool on a quarterly basis. Use Table 17.1 "Employee Self-Assessment of Job Challenge" to stay abreast of the employee's perception of the challenge in his or her work.

**Table 17.1**  Vulnerability Assessment Survey

| Employee: | | | | | | |
|---|---|---|---|---|---|---|
| **Part I:** | **Employee Self-Assessment of Job Challenge/Opportunity** | | | | | |
| **Category** | | **Strongly Agree** | **Agree** | **Neither Agree nor Disagree** | **Disagree** | **Strongly Disagree** |
| Challenge/Opportunity | | | | | | |
| 1. My work provides opportunties for my personal and professional growth. | | | | | | |
| 2. My management takes my technical growth and development into consideration when assigning work to me. | | | | | | |
| 3. I have a mentor who helps me improve my skills. | | | | | | |
| 4. My company provides training to improve my skills. | | | | | | |
| 5. After I return from training, I have an opportunity to practice what I've learned. | | | | | | |
| **TOTAL:** | | | | | | |

SOURCE: Copyright McGraw-Hill 2001. You may download this worksheet from *www.books. mcgraw-hill.com/training/download*. The document can then be opened, edited, and printed using Microsoft Word or other popular word-processing software.

**Table 17.2**  Scoring Suggestions for Employee Survey

| |
|---|
| 1. Review the answers to the statements provided by your employee. For every answer that the employee has scored in the last three columns, count this as a vulnerability factor. |
| 2. Total the number of vulnerability factors present. |
| 3. The higher the number of vulnerability factors present, the more likely it is that this employee will seek opportunities elsewhere. |

Table 17.3 contains a management analysis of other vulnerability factors. Make this a part of your monthly management process, and update it at least quarterly.

To evaluate the vulnerability of an employee, consider the following factors:

**Table 17.3**   Management Assessment of Employee Vulnerability

| Employee: | | | | | |
|---|---|---|---|---|---|
| **Part II:** | | | | | |
| Time in Job | < 1 Year | 1–2 Years | > 2–3 Years | > 3–5 Years | > 5 Years |
| Employee has been in the same job for: | | | | | |
| Training Days Per Year | > 5 Days | > 4–5 Days | > 2–4 Days | 1–2 Days | < 1 Day |
| Employee has received an average of ___ training this year. | | | | | |
| | | | | | |
| Check each culture change factor that applies to your company. | | | | | |
| Culture Changes | Company is reorganizing | | Company has been acquired by another company | | |
| | Company has been sold | | Company is restructuring or downsizing | | |
| | Company is merged with another company | | | | |
| Transition | Project or Assignment is coming to an end | | Mentor leaves company | | |
| | Sponsor leaves or is demoted | | Best friend leaves company | | |
| Changes at Home | Spouse is relocating to take another job | | Employee is having a child | | |
| | Family has purchased a home and is moving >25 miles from work | | Employee is getting married | | |
| | Employee is getting divorced | | Death/illness in family | | |
| Leadership | Employee has negative perception of manager, as indicated on surveys | | History of conflict with management | | |
| Compensation | Perceived pay inequity | | Employee's compensation hasn't kept pace with value in marketplace | | |
| Symptoms of Unrest | Loss of intensity | | Rumor mill has it that employee is "looking" | | |
| | Distancing self from co-workers | | Conflict with co-workers | | |
| | Change in employee's normal behavior | | Employee brings up compensation | | |

SOURCE: Copyright McGraw-Hill 2001. You may download this worksheet from *www.books. mcgraw-hill.com/training/download*. The document can then be opened, edited, and printed using Microsoft Word or other popular word-processing software.

## Challenge

In evaluating challenge consider the Employee Self-Assessment, the time the employee has been in the same job, and the average number of days of training each employee has received that year.

1. For the self-assessment, if your employee answered any of the five questions in columns 3–5, that probably indicates

some level of vulnerability due to the lack of perceived challenge in the job.

2. If time in job also falls in columns 4 or 5, consider that as a corroborating factor.
3. If days of training/year falls in columns 4 or 5 and the employee has self-assessed as needing challenge, consider this response as a corroborating factor.

### Change

In evaluating the impact of change on the employee, consider change to the company culture, transition in the employee's work, and changes at home.

If any of the above factors are checked within the category, consider change as a vulnerability factor for this employee.

### Leadership

If the employee has a negative perception of leadership or conflict with his/her manager, consider leadership as a vulnerability factor for this employee.

### Compensation

If the employee perceives a pay inequity or you know that the employee's compensation has not kept up with his/her skills in the marketplace, consider compensation a vulnerability factor for this employee.

### Symptoms

The symptoms listed suggested a change in mindset from one of satisfaction with the status quo to one of taking action to resolve the situation. If the employee displays any of the symptoms identified in the presence of other vulnerability factors, consider these as an accelerator.

Generally, the more factors that are present in your evaluation of a particular employee, the higher the degree of vulnerability.

The degree of vulnerability is not a direct correlation with an individual's propensity to turnover. Additionally, you will need to factor in the demand for the skills of the individual, their uniqueness in the marketplace, and the contribution to your company's mission to understand the true impact of turnover of this individual.

## Conclusion

1. Assess the vulnerability of your team members. Any employee exhibiting more than one factor should be targeted for immediate action.
2. If your company is going through a lot of change, take proactive steps to lessen the impact of change on your direct reports. Solicit employee involvement and input into the challenges and changes facing you. You may find that change can be the catalyst to galvanize the team to action.
3. Communicate openly and honestly with employees in transition. Provide support to those in need. Use adversity to shape loyalty.
4. Take action to improve your management skills. Consider training, mentorship, and coaching as ways to grow your skills. Ask employees for feedback. You will be surprised at the insights they can provide.
5. In spite of your best efforts some employees will still leave. Do not let it discourage you. Learn what you can from each defection by asking for candid feedback, and continue to steadily improve your organization.

# CHAPTER

## 18

# Creating a "Seriously Cool" Company Culture

Y OU'VE GONE to a great deal of trouble to attract them. Your business depends upon them. Everybody and his brother is trying to lure them away. So how can you keep them? This chapter explores the 3 C's of Keeping Winners:

- Character
- Culture
- Challenge

### Character

Have you ever worked for someone who says one thing and does another? For an organization that rewards not the best and brightest, but the most political? These are character defects— both individual and organizational. In Chapter 11 we discussed selecting for Character, because it makes good business sense. But, selecting employees for character and bringing them into an organization devoid of character is like inviting them to leave. Character breeds trust. And trust is at the heart of good client relationships. In our research into employee retention, 40 percent of the respondents wanted to work in an environment where there was mutual respect and trust among co-workers. They also wanted to work in an organization that was not "political". Trust breeds loyal employees. And loyalty among employees is a pre-requisite to customer loyalty.

In our research we asked people to choose the elements that described to them a "seriously cool" culture. Half of those responding chose principled leadership as the most important factor. Principled leadership is the kind of leadership that will do the right thing in spite of enormous pressure to do otherwise. Things you can do to show your character:

- Always hire for character, no exceptions.
- Infuse your vision statement with character values
- Derive operating principles that are character based and that empower every employee in the company to make character choices. For example, Digital Equipment Corporation (now Compaq) had a motto, *"Do The Right Thing"*. Employees were allowed to make decisions that would right a wrong created by mistakes or misapplication of policy. It was not unusual for a manager to give a customer credit in special circumstances. The policy not only bought good customer rapport; it also inspired the confidence of the management team in the company.
- Have a zero tolerance policy on breaches of company ethics
- Hold leadership to a high standard of excellence regarding character. Make it a major selection criterion. Reward leaders who uphold their principles under fire.
- Create a "Watch my Feet" award to be given monthly by employees to the team member that displays consistency in word and deed.

### Culture

Let's look at how the different cultures described in Chapter 9 might create attractive, "seriously cool" work climates. Remember, your culture may be unique to a workgroup, department, or team—or it could be a corporate culture. Your group's particular mission might dictate a unique culture. If that is the case, it is even more important that you be purposeful in sticking to those things that will create a winning culture for your workgroup.

### Lifestyle or Results

The lifestyle culture demonstrates consistency in making choices that reflect the value they place on the employee. This might look like a shortened workweek, or in-house child care; flexible work environments and work schedules. The message the lifestyle company sends to employees is *"You matter to us. We want to be important to you as well."* So, if you have a lifestyle culture...

- Create an employee involvement committee and empower them to develop their own recognition programs. Provide a budget and general guidelines, and allow the employees to decide how performance will be recognized.
- Solicit feedback about work hours and how client emergencies will be handled. Employees who value work/life balance want to meet client needs as well as others. Give them an opportunity to decide how to do so.
- Create "celebrations" of milestone achievements. Perhaps a pizza party, or an afternoon off. Let the entire work family participate in the success. Build a sense of shared accomplishment and esprit de corps.
- Celebrate personal milestones—birthdays, weddings, etc. It can be as simple as a circulated birthday card or a major bash.
- Consider involving the workers' extended family in celebrations of key milestones.
- Create a "Fun at Work" employee committee, and charter them to come up with ideas to increase the fun at work.

Beware—if you call yourself a lifestyle company but consistently make decisions that ask the employee to sacrifice work/life balance in favor of a more pressing company commitment—you will lose employees. It's okay once in a while to require sacrifice of personal time to meet a business need, but when it becomes routine, you are not being honest about your culture. The key to success in a lifestyle culture is employee involvement. Keep them involved in the day to day running of the company, and you will keep them.

If you are a results-based culture, you will have to compensate more aggressively for the sacrifices and stresses that accompany this work style. Companies that fit this profile fall into three categories. At the top of the financial pecking order are the dot coms, with their aggressive equity packages. Next come the high flying financial institutions with their six and seven figure compensation packages, and then the third tier would be those companies who are results based and willing to compensate in the top 75 percentile. In an achievement-oriented culture you might:

- Create visible reminders of performance, both on an individual and group basis.
- Rank and publish employee performance statistics, and provide frequent feedback and recognition for goal attainment.
- Develop compensation programs with levers for over-achievement of goals.
- Offer monetary rewards for bringing in programs that exceed profitability goals, or designing solutions that meet client milestones.
- Consider offering an equity position to employees. The value of the employee's investment in the company increases with overall company performance.
- Tie all company communication to the results theme.

Lehman Brothers effectively straddles the two extremes of a results-based culture that also respects personal motivations. Kevin McGilloway, Chief Information Officer and Managing Director of Lehman Brothers, believes that people are motivated by what he calls "PPF—a balancing act between one's personal, professional, and financial motivations." He stresses with his management team that there is no one PPF equation. Different individuals within Lehman value different aspects of it. Some people seek a high financial reward; for others it is a balance between the quality of their personal lives and financial rewards. Some seek flexibility in their workplace. McGilloway challenges his management team to come up with innovative ways of customizing the PPF across the various geographies, cultures, and locations.

## Technology vs. Market Focus

The implied assumption in the technology-focused culture is *"If you build a better mousetrap, people will beat a path to your door."* The implied assumption in the market-focused culture is *"A mediocre product strategy, well-executed, will beat a superior product with a poorly-executed strategy every time."* Techies who value keeping their skills current will naturally be drawn to the technology-focused company. But if your culture is market-focused, don't despair. In our research, only 25 percent of the participants listed "hot technology" as part of a seriously cool culture. So, although hot technology appeals to a number of people, it is not the only factor to draw techies to a given company. If your company is technology-focused...

- Create a "sand box"—a technical area where workers can experiment with leading-edge relevant technology.
- Create "Centers of Excellence"—either physical or virtual worlds where employees discuss technology trends and suggest solutions.
- Reward and recognize both technical breadth and depth.
- Offer coupons redeemable for tech training.
- Set up a peer recognition program that identifies technical contribution.
- Reward contributions that lead to product innovation with equity or cash.

If yours is a market-focused environment...

- Reward employees based on positive customer feedback, contract extension or renewal.
- Develop mottos that speak to the importance of a satisfied customer.
- Make customer satisfaction a key measurement in all reward and recognition programs.

## Innovation or Process

The company that is primarily process-driven will tend to look inward and apply structure and method to assure consistency.

If your company is process-driven...

- Reward and recognize consistent application of methodology to the way employees accomplish their work.
- Establish a learning culture. In our research 44 percent of the respondents saw a Learning Culture as an integral part of a "seriously cool" culture. Use project/program reviews as opportunities for learning. Give a prize for the best mistake. Absolutely refuse to allow mistakes to be punished.
- Recognize consistency in achievement.
- Employ mentors to help new employees learn methodology.
- Build a management process that revolves around the methodology.
- Select people who are comfortable in a more structured environment.

The company that is driven by innovation looks outward at the market and may feel the need to reconceptualize itself as the market shifts. If your company is primarily innovation driven...

- Offer equity for the best new idea of the month, quarter, year—whatever timeframe works in your organization.
- Recognize and value the people who have the best ideas.
- Use the brainstorm, and other techniques that surface creativity to motivate the organization.
- Keep your environment casual. Allow for individuality of expression. If you have a group of web designers, give a prize (employee awarded) for the most creative cubicle.
- Use the sandbox idea—create a space for tech exploration.
- Offer as a perq training on a technology that the person values.

## Challenge

No matter what the culture, challenging work is one of the most important reasons why people both join and stay with a company. People are looking for work that has meaning, that makes a difference, that makes a contribution. When asked why they were in the business of consulting, and what motivated them, a group of consultants said... *"To go where no man has gone before. To explore new territories."* Techies are motivated by learning new things. People are looking for a culture that fosters learning and for work where they can fully utilize their talents. Challenge comes in many forms. Some challenge is in the work itself. Other challenge comes in the form of training and development. To keep challenge in your workplace...

- **Rotate people** into jobs or roles that offer significant challenge. Use job rotation as an opportunity to develop new skills.
- **Don't allow an employee to linger too long in a role that has become "old."** Research supports that the longer an employee has been in one job, the higher probability of turnover.
- **Give newcomers significant roles and responsibilities.** Provide "safety nets" in the form of coaches and mentors to maintain quality of output. You will be pleasantly surprised at the results. Young hotshots continually tell us that they feel underutilized. Use 'em or lose 'em.
- **Create a business challenge committee.** Make it a forum where your best and brightest get to chew on some of the weightiest issues facing your company. G.E. uses a similar concept to test the mettle of its high potentials. The executive committee of the company reviews the output of this committee, providing both visibility for the high potentials and a forum for exchange of new ideas.
- **Encourage cross-company, cross-division movement of people.** Too often a manager will hold onto a promising person rather than lose the person to another division. What inevitably happens is that the company loses the person to another company that will put them in play.
- **Reach way down into the organization** to identify high potential employees early in their careers. The CEO of a Fortune 50 company commented that with his traditional high potential program by the time a high potential was identified, it was too late in his or her career for them to have some pivotal developmental experiences. "Casting a wider net and reaching employees earlier in their careers allowed us to be very planful about pivotal work experiences," he says.

# What's the World's Best Retention Tool? (Hint: It's Not Money.)

THE WORLD'S BEST retention tool is sitting in your chair right now. Your effectiveness as a leader probably has more to do with keeping talent on board than any other single thing. Knowing this, we asked tech workers what constituted good and bad leadership. The most frequently cited example of bad leadership was *"I couldn't trust him/her,"* the next was *"Concerned only about him/herself."* Slightly behind this was a manager who *"micro-managed me."* Conversely, they described the **best boss** they ever had as someone who *"helped me grow", "supported me,"* and *"pushed me to do my best."*

Reflecting on this data, if a company were to identify the most important single retention tool, then it would be the character of its leadership. The second most important thing a leader can do is to help his or her employees to grow, to challenge them and push them to do their best. This chapter explores the most effective leadership behavior styles in technology-driven businesses and offers practical suggestions you can begin to implement today.

Let's assume you've read this book and applied the principles we've suggested. Before you hired your people you created a staffing plan, then using your ideal hire profile you chose people wisely and successfully wooed and won them. They said "yes", and now you are working together in a marriage of sorts. But, just as the courtship is not over when you walk down the aisle, neither is the job of "winning" your top talent. Because weekly—if not daily—your employees are besieged with siren calls to lure them away. You are effectively watching the door with an vulnerability warning system lest anyone should rethink his or her decision to join your team. You are doing your best to create the kind of place where people want to stay. But, is that all there is? Well, not quite.

Having spent many years consulting on executive development, and having assessed and coached literally hundreds of executives in some of the country's most successful companies, we still marvel at the fact that the executive is by far the most underleveraged resource in any company. In Chapter 4, as we discussed the concept of the Superstar, we emphasized the importance of selecting them very carefully because of the enormous influence they would have. This is equally true of you as a leader. When we conduct dialogues with leadership groups, one of the most important concepts we drive home is the extent of the power and influence of a leader who chooses to use it. Inevitably, in such a workshop, the recurring theme that emerges is *"if it wasn't for them, we'd be great."* Inevitably the *"them"* is someone else in the organization, usually higher in the organization. Unless our dialogue is with the CEO, then the *"them"* may flow to his or her leadership team or to the Board of Directors. But what we find is that for whatever reason leaders are not willing or able to *"own"* their power to shape events.

But research shows that when the leadership of the company takes ownership of employee retention and focuses on it, employees stay. So what does good technology leadership look like, and what are some things that you can do today to help shape your company into a talent magnet?

## A model for technology leadership

Table 19.1 represents a model for successful technology leadership, and contains some suggestions for things you can do to demonstrate good leadership to your employees.

**Table 19.1** Technology Leadership Success Profile

| Character | | | |
|---|---|---|---|
| **Learning** | **Analyzing** | **Relating** | **Performing** |
| Active learning | Technical acumen | Perceptiveness | Sense of urgency |
| Knowledge transfer | Business acumen | Influence | Execution |
| Developing others | Problem solving | Collaboration | Drive to achieve |
| | Decisiveness | Customer insight | Accomplishment |
| | | | Optimism |

### Character

Our research indicates that character is by far the most important, most consistent attribute of leadership. Think of character as sitting in the center of a diamond shape. At each of the points of the diamond sit the other capabilities—learning, analyzing, relating, and performing. The more strength a leader possesses in a given capability, the stronger the points on the diamond, and the stronger your character, the more solid the center of the diamond. However, the shape of one's character really defines how the world sees you. You can be brilliant at all of the other capabilities, but if you are character-deficient, then you have a "hole" in the middle of your leadership profile—the weaker your character, the bigger the hole eaten into your profile. So it doesn't matter how talented you are in other areas if you are deficient in character. People will see you as a person of character by the way you handle yourself. If you want to demonstrate character be...

- Accountable: Accept a *"the buck stops here"* approach to business issues. Even if you delegate a task to others, you are still ultimately accountable for the results. Empower others, delegating responsibility appropriately.
- Consistent: Your people need to know how you will react to events. Given similar situations there is a comfort to be derived from knowing that you will react the same way to the same stimuli. Your predictability will generate stability. This means that if you had an argument with your significant other before you left the house, you do not bring that tension with you. It also means that if your boss just chewed you out, you do not pass on inappropriate tension. Just

because someone else has managed you badly doesn't mean you need to emulate it.

- Courageous: People follow and are attracted to leaders who show courage in the face of adversity. The knowledge that your people can count on you to stand up for a principle will energize them and foster loyalty. This means you protect your people from injustices. If, for example, you made an agreement with an employee, keep your word.

- Principled: Take actions based upon a set of principles or standards. Be courageous in upholding them. Let people know what your principles are. They embue your organization with consistency. Principles generate empowerment. If your employees know your principles and are empowered to make decisions according to them, you have freed your team up to act. The more clarity you can bring to the principles by which you will run the business, the better your organization will run. This works especially well if your team has derived a set of guiding principles together. You get tremendous ownership from the process.

- Candid: Be frank and honest in dealing with others. If you are not at liberty to disclose something, tell people your situation. Do not attempt to hide it. It comes off as dishonesty. People want to work with someone they can trust.

- Trustworthy: Demonstrate consistency between your words and actions. Walk the talk. Be free from any deception. There is nothing that drains productivity more than a discrepancy between words and deeds.

- Constant: Stay the course. Act steadfastly, even in adversity. The ability to keep a steady hand at the till when the winds of change are blowing so strongly they can capsize the ship—that's true leadership in action. It can look like an email to the team to encourage them after they've just lost an order. Or an after-hours heart-to-heart with a team member who has just suffered a personal setback.

- Genuine: Be yourself. They know you anyway.

- Just: Be fair and reasonable. Apply your principles in a logical and equitable way. When you do this, everyone will know and respect you for your principles.

## Learning

Like other talented people, the leader is a quick study, but that is not what distinguishes him or her from the rest. The leader who wants to retain his or her people is very concerned about their personal growth and development. To retain your people...

- Focus on career development. Initiate career counseling discussions with your team members. Understand what motivates them, where they want to be in two years, in five. Plan with them to make it happen at your company, or they will make it happen on their own.
- Push them to their limit—and beyond. The managers people remember as being the best are the ones that continually challenged them to become better, more competent. It may have felt uncomfortable when it was happening, but employees appreciate challenge.
- Be a coach. Either personally or by utilizing others, establish a coaching structure. Give people support as they grow.
- Drive organizational learning. Create an environment where mistakes are celebrated as opportunities to learn. Draw on the skills of the entire team to continually improve.

## Analyzing

The leader is typically strong in all of the analyzing capabilities. Strength in problem solving and critical thinking fosters exploration of the unknown or ambiguous. To use your analyzing ability to retain people...

- Take the strategic view. Understand—and communicate to others—the long-term implications of decisions.
- Continually involve others in solving complex problems. Build a sense of shared ownership in solving a problem. Help them understand the principle of unintended consequences by exploring unintended consequences of differing solution alternatives.
- Explore problems together. The best way to describe this is visually. You want to create the kind of feeling that you are

both on the same side of the desk looking at the problem together. That perspective changes everything.

- Develop the business acumen of your technical team. Not all techies will be drawn to understand the business implications of technical decisions. Continually broaden their understanding of not only the technology but the business environment within which it operates. Help them understand how value is created and they will create value for you. Teach them to recognize and act on opportunities that can have a sustained effect on the organization.

### Relating

The ability to interact successfully with others, to see others, to communicate effectively and use influence to shape events is a strong leadership capability. Your ability to relate to others is one of the attributes that allowed you to become a leader. Use your ability to relate to...

- Develop a rapport with the members of your team. Know where they hang out. Know what makes them tick.
- The team is the thing... Foster teamwork and shared problem solving. Reward and recognize behavior that is conducive to team unity.
- Communicate, communicate, communicate. Your team may not be very vocal, but that doesn't mean they don't want you to communicate with them. Because your team is a technical one, the precision in your wording is very important. This team sees distinctions that a less technical team might not see. Say exactly what you mean. This team can be inspired. They don't want to be "sold."
- Show them that you care. They won't care how much you know until they know how much you care.
- Teach them to be better communicators. Work on the communication skills of your team. They will thank you for it.

### Performing

The leader performs, and inspires his or her team to perform. Although different cultures place different value on performance, all companies must perform. The only issue is in how you achieve your goals. The results-based cultures will use rewards and recognition to drive performance; whereas, the relationship-based cultures will emphasize more employee involvement in results attainment. To encourage performance...

- Be optimistic. Events will at times conspire to defeat you. Turn that defeat into either a learning experience or an opportunity to persevere until success is the result. Keep the spirit of the team up and you will keep turnover down.
- Foster a sense of urgency. Expect milestones to be met. Hold people accountable, just as you expect to be held accountable. Focus on action, not thrashing. Whenever the team gets paralyzed by indecision, come up with an action-based approach to break the logjam.
- Support teamwork in meeting goals. Goal attainment is important. But the person who "breaks glass" while attaining goals is only getting it half right. Help people understand what it means to execute as a team.

### Give me a lever big enough ...

Archimedes said, *"Give me a lever big enough and I can move the world."* In your company, you are the lever, and your effectiveness in moving your world is a reflection of your effectiveness as a leader. Leaders represent the most underdeveloped assets in any company, yet they are many times more valuable than capital assets. Commit today to develop this asset. Commit today that you will devote time and energy to develop your leadership ability, just as you continue to grow your technical team. The more effective you become, the bigger your lever.

# APPENDIX

# Staffing Plan Examples

## CYA Technologies Staffing Plan

CYA TECHNOLOGIES, INC. is headquartered in Trumbull, CT and develops software products and utilities for Web content management systems that are sold directly and through a select global partner program. Founded in 1998, CYA Technologies' client list has grown to include some of the largest pharmaceutical and manufacturing companies in the world, while the company itself has remained privately held and relatively small. The company's plans for 2000 include hiring an additional 75 employees, primarily to fill positions in the technical services area. To facilitate this, the company has partnered with staffing firms that understand the long-term goals of the company, upgraded equipment to entice the technically savvy, created a casual atmosphere that encourages learning and allows members to take active parts in projects that are decidedly out of their usual niche. The chemistry and experience of the team is the driving force behind the success of the company.

**Table A.I**   CYA Technologies Staffing Plan

# Staffing Plan

| | |
|---|---|
| **Manager:**  Bruce Brainstorm | **Department:**   Technical Development |

*Step 1:  Understand the goals of your corporate strategy.*

ACTION:  Identify the main goals of your corporate strategy:

| Goal ID. | Corporate Goal Description |
|---|---|
| #1 | To reach ~75 employees by year-end: This is a critical step in the company achieving its full potential.  The bulk of these employees are going to be part of the development team, they need to be sharp, innovative, and dedicated in order to reach the goals put forth by marketing and management, which capitalize on the current market and growing trends. |
| #2 | To go public by 2002: This is the goal of every team member. Going public means that we've achieved our goals and adhered to our strategy of bringing in quality employees who understand the vision. |

*Step 2:  Describe your workgroup's goals and the structure you will need to achieve them.*

ACTIONS:
(A) List the goals of your workgroup in the column entitled "Workgroup Goal Description".
(B) List your plan to achieve each goal in the column entitled "Plan to Achieve".
(C) Insert or attach a copy of the proposed organization chart that you will use to achieve your goals.
(D) List the roles (Example:  Project Manager) you will need in the column entitled "Identified Workgroup Roles", and identify whether you (1) already have them, (2) plan to grow them or (3) buy them in the appropriate columns.

| A. Workgroup Goal Description | B. Plan to Achieve |
|---|---|
| Develop Product "Teams" | Hire three more Technical Leads who will lead teams of about 4-5 developers |
| Commercially release at least four new products in 2001 | Break existing talent into groups so that they can tackle a more focused and rigorous development schedule rather than overwhelming existing team with several tasks at once |

**C. Organization: CYA Product Team**

**Table A.I** CYA Technologies Staffing Plan *(Continued)*

| D. Identified Workgroup Roles | Have | Grow | Buy |
|---|---|---|---|
| Chief of Technical Operations | X | | |
| Technical Lead | X | | |
| Technical Lead | | | X |
| Technical Lead | | | X |
| Technical Lead | | | X |
| Developers (~16) | X (3) | X (1) | X (~12) |
| Quality Assurance Manager | X (1) | | X (1) |
| QA Specialists | X (2) | | X (2) |
| QA Analysts | | | X (4) |

*Step 3: Evaluate your current talent.*

A. Evaluate employee contribution to goal attainment.

| Employee Name | Describe Contribution to Mission | Describe Uniqueness of Skills | Quadrant |
|---|---|---|---|
| Bruce Brainstorm | Has the future product schedule and current product information ideas | This member of the team is a critical component and has the vision, intelligence, drive, and people skills to get the company to the next level. | Super Star |
| Dan Development | Intended to lead a team in the development of specific software solutions | This member should have a high degree of technical and managerial skills, a rare combination in the technical field | Heavy Hitter |
| Corinne Coder | This member must be able to catch on fast and ensure that all products adhere to the development schedule. | There are many people today with this skill set, however, we require that they have good people skills and a passion for the niche in which we function | Specialists |
| Quality Quinn | This member is needed to ensure that the products meet quality standards. This work must be done quickly and thoroughly. | There are not many people in the market-place that opt for Quality Assurance over Development. Good People can be found but with time | Specialist |
| | | | |
| | | | |
| | | | |
| | | | |

**Table A.I**   CYA Technologies Staffing Plan *(Continued)*

B. Consider employee growth potential

| Employee Name | Current Quadrant | Potential to Move To | Actions Needed |
|---|---|---|---|
| Peggy Programmer | Worker bee | Specialist | Continue to involve Peggy in more challenging projects and listen to her needs. She is transitioning from one department to another and shows a lot of potential |
| Sally Server | Specialist | Heavy Hitter | Sally is very bright and has excellent people skills. The deciding factor will depend on how often we can get Sally in front of clients and how successful she is working closely with them |

*Step 4: Plan for succession.*

A. Identify key vacancies in your workgroup/department/division/organization, by listing job titles in the appropriate blanks.

| Workgroup Openings | Department Openings | Division Openings | Organization Openings |
|---|---|---|---|
| Technical Leads | | | |
| | | | |
| | | | |

B. Map current employees into potential openings

| Job Title | Location | Candidate | Projected to Fill By |
|---|---|---|---|
| Sally Server | Development | Technical Lead | Q2 2001 |
| | | | |
| | | | |

C. Identify vacancies created by employee promotions

| Job Title | Location | Projected Date of Vacancy |
|---|---|---|
| Senior Developer | Development | Q2 2001 |
| | | |
| | | |

**Table A.1**  CYA Technologies Staffing Plan *(Continued)*

D. Identify gaps to be sourced outside of company.

| Job Title | Number of Vacancies | Location | Date |
|---|---|---|---|
| Technical Leads | 2 | Technical Services | ASAP |
| Developers | ~12 | Technical Services | ASAP |
| Quality Assurance Manager | 1 | Technical Services | ASAP |
| Quality Assurance Analyst | 4 | Technical Services | ASAP |
| Quality Assurance Specialist | 2 | Technical Services | ASAP |

*Step 5: Anticipate Attrition.*

ACTION:
Identify the employees that you feel may be considering leaving the company, indicating the value of their contribution (by Quadrant) and anticipated attrition date.

| Employee | Role | Quadrant | Vulnerability Indicator | Projected Attrition Date |
|---|---|---|---|---|
| N/A | | | | |
| | | | | |
| | | | | |

*Step 6: Determine Hiring Specifications*

ACTION: Prioritize the vacancies you would like to have filled by quarter.

| Job Title | Number of Vacancies | Quarter to Fill |
|---|---|---|
| Technical Leads | 4 | Q1/01 |
| Developers | 12 | Q2/01 |

*Step 7: Develop Sourcing Strategy*

A. Bring forward Culture description from Chapter 9, and identify your value proposition.

| Culture Description | Value Proposition |
|---|---|
| CYA Technologies falls under the Innovation category quite clearly. We are company that does not like structure or rigid guidelines and our team is comprised of members that tend to work best alone or on the fly, learning new things as they go. The value of this culture to our company is that we are able to adapt quickly, stay on the cutting-edge of technology and are always ready, often waiting, for change. It's perfect for our industry which is in a constant state of flux. | |

**Table A.I** CYA Technologies Staffing Plan *(Continued)*

| |
|---|
| B. Identify any other constraints that will affect your ability to source. |

There are three major constraints affecting our ability to source. These constraints are time, money, and compatibility.

**TIME:** In order for the company to achieve certain goals set in our business plan, we must adhere to a schedule. Because of this we a faced with the following problem: Do we adhere to the schedule and fill spaces, or do we risk missing "key" milestones to hold out for just the right hire? To date, we've been lucky. We've held out and reaped the rewards, but how long can that go on before the effect is damaging? We may need to begin an aggressive effort to just fill up critical spaces in order to hit the market right and maintain our current momentum and steady revenue growth.

**MONEY:** Money is another critical component when trying to build a quality team. As a younger company, it can at times be difficult to compete with larger, more established firms. It is a difficult situation when employees that have been with you for a long time and have sacrificed hours and possibly even pay to help build a company, suddenly find that in order to attract new hires, starting salaries must be higher. Here again is a problem, how does a company attract new help without alienating existing staff and how does the company ensure that these dollars, now coming from investment money, are being wisely used in the overall strategy to make the company grow?

There is a fine line here between success and failure. If older, loyal employees feel that they are not given what is due to them, they may walk, taking with them not only knowledge that the company can't replace, but the personalities that have created the corporate culture that has proven successful, creating an environment that may become "dull". In other words, that entreprenurial drive that we looked for in every employee early on and helped shape the company, may be lost because we've sacrificed it for quick hires.

**COMPATABILITY:** In addition to time and money limiting how quickly we can source candidates, a good fit with our corporate culture is just as important if not more than technical expertise. Since we work in a fast-paced environment, team members must be quick on their feet, able to take criticism in stride

| |
|---|
| C. Based on your culture, value proposition, and other constraints, what will be your strategy for sourcing candidates? |

The company strategy for sourcing candidates is two pronged. We will be using aggressive head-hunters to lure the most qualified candidates into the Heavy Hitter positions. However, even those who have stellar qualifications may not be right for our team and so we employ an aggressive interview process in which many different team members get the opportunity to meet the candidate and determine if he is an appropriate addition.

For specialty or worker bee positions, we have had success with job fairs and want ads. In our area, we benefit from the demise of New York and Boston dot.coms, so there are usually enough people to fill less specialized areas. Again, we are looking for intelligence and personality so first impressions are very valuable. If someone clearly doesn't fit into our environment, we are not shy about letting them know as it saves both our time and theirs.

Of course, a company full of people who loathe structure and strive to buck the system may not be the most sensible way to achieve goals, so there are a few people mixed in who may be described as conservative but who also possess excellent people and managerial skills and so the team meshes nicely and leverages each others strong qualities.

**Table A.2** New Jersey State Police MDC Project Staffing Plan

| Staffing Plan | |
|---|---|
| **Manager:** | **Department:** |

*Step 1: Understand the goals of your corporate strategy.*

ACTION: Identify the main goals of your corporate strategy:

| Goal ID. | Corporate Goal Description |
|---|---|
| | Provide Troopers with mobile data computers (MDCs) in their patrol vehicles, facilitating on-line reporting capabilities, and providing instant access to criminal justice databases. |

*Step 2: Describe your workgroup's goals and the structure you will need to achieve them.*

ACTIONS:
(A) List the goals of your workgroup in the column entitled "Workgroup Goal Description".
(B) List your plan to achieve each goal in the column entitled "Plan to Achieve".
(C) Insert or attach a copy of the proposed organization chart that you will use to achieve your goals.
(D) List the roles (Example: Project Manager) you will need in the column entitled "Identified Workgroup Roles", and identify whether you (1) already have them, (2) plan to grow them or (3) buy them in the appropriate columns.

| A. Workgroup Goal Description | B. Plan to Achieve |
|---|---|
| Develop MDC Software | Create a Project Team to handle the development and ongoing maintenance/enhancement of the MDC software. The team will basically be divided into two areas of development: GUI/Client-side processing and Communications/Server-side processing. In addition, the team will be augmented with an IT architect. The architect's job will be to research and document options, and recommend a macro-level solution to the project manager. He/She will also provide the other team members with assistance as necessary. |
| Establish support infrastructure | Expand the existing Installation and Repair Unit to be able to support over 800 MDCs which will be deployed throughout the state. The Unit must be able to bring support to the MDCs on a 24 by 7 basis, and be able to resolve any problem within two hours. In order to accomplish this, three areas of responsibility will be created to service the northern, central, and southern regions of the state. Personnel will be assigned to three regional offices, and will work under the direction of a regional supervisor. It will be the job of the regional supervisor to coordinate his/her efforts with the Unit Head. Service calls will be handled by an existing Help Desk, and escalated to the regional support personnel when necessary. |

**Table A.2** New Jersey State Police MDC Project Staffing Plan
*(Continued)*

**C. Organization:**

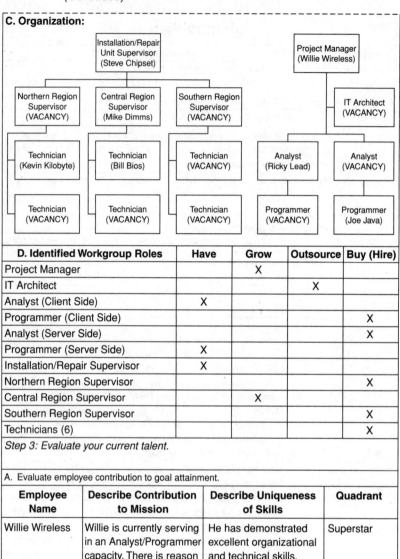

| D. Identified Workgroup Roles | Have | Grow | Outsource | Buy (Hire) |
|---|---|---|---|---|
| Project Manager | | X | | |
| IT Architect | | | X | |
| Analyst (Client Side) | X | | | |
| Programmer (Client Side) | | | | X |
| Analyst (Server Side) | | | | X |
| Programmer (Server Side) | X | | | |
| Installation/Repair Supervisor | X | | | |
| Northern Region Supervisor | | | | X |
| Central Region Supervisor | | X | | |
| Southern Region Supervisor | | | | X |
| Technicians (6) | | | | X |

*Step 3: Evaluate your current talent.*

A. Evaluate employee contribution to goal attainment.

| Employee Name | Describe Contribution to Mission | Describe Uniqueness of Skills | Quadrant |
|---|---|---|---|
| Willie Wireless | Willie is currently serving in an Analyst/Programmer capacity. There is reason to believe that Willie is looking at other opportunities, and he should be retained at all cost. | He has demonstrated excellent organizational and technical skills, and contributes beyond all expectations. | Superstar |

**Table A.2**  New Jersey State Police MDC Project Staffing Plan
*(Continued)*

| | | | |
|---|---|---|---|
| Ricky Lead | Ricky does a good job as an Analyst/Programmer, but he's no ball of fire. The rumor mill says he's dissatisfied with his current assignment, and is actively looking for other opportunities. | He does not possess any specialized skills and his contributions are just ordinary. | Worker Bee |
| Joe Java | Joe has excellent Java programming skills. He has been an outstanding contributer in the past, and has an insatiable desire to learn new programming techniques. | He loves challenging work and wants to remain a programmer. | Superstar |
| Steve Chipset | Steve has been around for a long time and he's done an excellent job with a small staff. Steve has a motor that just won't stop, but he doesn't possess any irreplaceable skills. He'll have to move away from the technical stuff, and learn to become more of a manager. | Steve's knowledge could be replaced, but it would be difficult to find someone as hard working as him. | Heavy Hitter |
| Harry Harddrive | Harry has little experience as a computer technician, but his educational background is fairly impressive. | He has an excellent rapport with the other unit members and has shown a lot of promise (e.g., organizational skills, innovation, etc.) | Specialist |
| Mike Dimms | Mike has been our "go to" guy for a little over two years. When all else fails, people go to him for answers. | His technical skills are excellent, and his contributions are great. | Superstar |
| Bill Bios | Bill's technical skills are just average. His contributions are barely adequate, and experience has shown that his work needs to be monitored closely. | He has done little to stay current with technological advancements. | Worker Bee |
| Kevin Kilobyte | Kevin picks things up very quickly and has good technical skills. He finishes his assignment with little supervision, but he doesn't go out of his way to look for work. | | Worker Bee |

**Table A.2** New Jersey State Police MDC Project Staffing Plan
*(Continued)*

B. Consider employee growth potential

| Employee Name | Current Quadrant | Potential to Move To | Actions Needed |
|---|---|---|---|
| Willie Wireless | Superstar | Superstar | Project Management Training |
| Ricky Lead | Worker Bee | Specialist | Technical training |
| Joe Java | Superstar | Superstar | Keep him challenged |
| Steve Chipset | Heavy Hitter | Superstar | Management training |
| Harry Harddrive | Specialist | Superstar | Technical training |
| Mike Dimms | Superstar | Superstar | Management training |
| Bill Bios | Worker Bee | Specialist | Technical training, Coaching |
| Kevin Kilobyte | Worker Bee | Heavy Hitter | Coaching |

*Step 4: Plan for succession.*

A. Identify key vacancies in your workgroup/department/division/organization, by listing job titles in the appropriate blanks.

| Workgroup Openings | Department Openings | Division Openings | Organization Openings |
|---|---|---|---|
| Project Manager (1) | MDC Project | | |
| IT Architect (1) | MDC Project | | |
| Analysts (2) | MDC Project | | |
| Programmers (2) | MDC Project | | |
| Assistant Unit Supervisor(1) | Installation/Repair Unit | | |
| Regional Supervisors (3) | Installation/Repair Unit | | |
| Technicians (4) | Installation/Repair Unit | | |

B. Map current employees into potential openings

| Job Title | Location | Candidate | Projected to Fill By |
|---|---|---|---|
| Project Manager | MDC Project | Willie Wireless | Jan 2001 |
| Analyst | MDC Project | Ricky Lead | Jan 2001 |
| Programmer | MDC Project | Joe Java | Jan 2001 |
| Assistant Unit Supervisor | Installation/Repair Unit | Harry Harddrive | Jan 2001 |
| Central Region Supervisor | Installation/Repair Unit | Mike Dimms | Jan 2001 |

C. Identify vacancies created by employee promotions

| Job Title | Location | Projected Date of Vacancy |
|---|---|---|
| (2) Analysts | Maintenance Team | Jan 2001 |
| Programmer | Maintenance Team | Jan 2001 |
| | | |

D. Identify gaps (vacancies) to be sourced from outside of company.

| Job Title | Number of Vacancies | Location | Date |
|---|---|---|---|
| IT Architect | 1 | MDC Project | September 2000 |
| Analyst | 1 | MDC Project | January 2001 |
| Programmer | 1 | MDC Project | January 2001 |
| Northern Region Supervisor | 1 | Installation/Repair Unit | June 2001 |
| Southern Region Supervisor | 1 | Installation/Repair Unit | June 2001 |
| Technician | 4 | Installation/Repair Unit | June 2001 |

**Table A.2** New Jersey State Police MDC Project Staffing Plan
*(Continued)*

---

*Step 5: Anticipate attrition.*

ACTION:
Identify the employees that you feel may be considering leaving the company, indicating the value of their contribution (by Quadrant) and anticipated attrition date.

| Employee | Role | Quadrant | Vulnerability Indicator | Projected Attrition Date |
|----------|------|----------|-------------------------|--------------------------|
| None |  |  |  |  |
|  |  |  |  |  |
|  |  |  |  |  |

*Step 6: Determine hiring specifications*

ACTION: Prioritize the vacancies you would like to have filled by quarter.

| Job Title | Number of Vacancies | Quarter to Fill |
|-----------|---------------------|-----------------|
|  |  |  |

*Step 7: Develop candidate sourcing strategy*

A. Bring forward Culture description from Chapter 9, and identify your value proposition.

| Culture Description | Value Proposition |
|---------------------|-------------------|
|  |  |

B. Identify any other constraints that will affect your ability to source.

|  |
|--|
|  |
|  |

C. Based on your culture, value proposition, and other constraints, what will be your strategy for sourcing candidates?

|  |
|--|
|  |

# Endnotes

## Introduction

1. U.S. Department of Labor, Bureau of Labor Statistics, "The Digital Work Force: Building Infotech Skills at the Speed of Innovation." June, 1999.

## Chapter 3

1. Business Special Report: 7th Annual 100 Best Places to Work in IT". *Computerworld*. June 5, 2000.
2. Ueem, Jerry. "For Sale Online: You". *Fortune*. July 5, 1999.
3. Pipeline. Contract Professional. March, 2000.
4. Useem, Jerry. "Read This Before You Put a Resume Online". *Fortune*, May 24, 1999.
5. Abramson, Gary. "(Your Boss) Heard It Through the Grapevine". *CIO Enterprise*, Section 2. April 15, 1999.
6. Laver, Ross. "Recruiting on the Web: In a highly competitive labour market, employers are turning to the Net to find new people". *Maclean's*. May 29, 2000.
7. Battey, Jim. Enterprise Careers: The keys to recruiting success, Vol. 22. InfoWorld. February 28, 2000.
8. Operation Transition. *http://www.dmdc.osd.mil/ot/ot*
9. 1999 Electronic Recruiting Index. *http://www.interbiznet.com*
10. Hollander, Bret. Sourcerer's Apprentice. May, June, and July 2000. *http://www.netcruiter.com*
11. McGee, Marianne Kolbasuk and Greenemeier, Larry. "Lifestyle Location", *informationweek.com*. May 29, 2000.
12. Hyman, Julie. "Technology firms fish for recruits in unusual waters". *The Washington Times*. February 23, 2000.
13. United States Department of Labor, Training Technology Research Center Web site. *http://www.ttrcnew.ttrc.doleta.gov/common/directories*

## Chapter 4

1. Perlow, Leslie—"Boundary control: the social ordering of work and family time in a high-tech corporation". Cornell University. Vol. 43. *Administrative Science Quarterly*. June 1, 1998.

2. Behilling, Orlando. "Employee selection: will intelligence and conscientiousness do the job?" Vol. 12, *The Academy of Management Executive*. February 1, 1998.
3. Epstein, Miles Z., and Epstein, David G. "Hiring Veterans: A cost-effective staffing solution in today's tight labor market, hiring the men and women who are leaving the military can save your company more than $100,000 per year in search". *HR Magazine*. November 1, 1998.
4. Clay, Rebecca A. "Many managers frown on use of flexible work options". *APA Monitor*, American Psychological Association. Vol. 29, No. 7. July, 1998.

## Chapter 6

1. "Will Work for Millions", *Business Week Frontier*. April 24, 2000.
2. Salter, Chuck. "Talent—Jeff Daniel". *FastCompany*. December 1, 1999.
3. Merrill, Kevin. "CRN Business Weekly: IT Managers Send SOS—Qualified Help Wanted"...*Computers Reseller* News. April 19, 1999.
4. Martinez, Michelle Neely. How Top Recruiters Snag New Grads. *HR Magazine*. August 1, 1997.
5. Buckman, Rebecca. "What Price a BMW? At Stanford, it may only cost a resume". *Wall Street Journal*. May 19, 2000.
6. Evans, Bob and Soat, John. "Who What, Where: The IT Landscape". *Information Week*. May 29, 2000.
7. Kroll, Karen M. "Catch a Rising Star". *Industry Week*. March 6, 2000.
8. Oleck, Joan. Frontier: "Invasion of the Body Snatchers". *Business Week*. Vol. 3650. October 11, 1999.
9. No Author Available. "New Fee Structures Change Executive Search Landscape—Goodbye to the Sacred 33%?" *Business Wire*. February 2, 1999.
10. Falcone, Paul. "Maximize Your Recruitment Resources: Matching the type of agency to fit your needs can save time, money". *HR Magazine*. February 1, 1999.
11. Sellers, Patricia. "These People Would Like to Stalk, Capture and Sell You. Perhaps You Should Let Them". *ecompany*. June 2000.
12. Author Not Available. "79% of Global 500 Recruiting on Corporate Web Sites". *Business Wire*. May 10, 2000.

## Chapter 9

1. Cameron, Kim S, and Quinn, Robert E., "Diagnosing and Changing Organizational Culture: Based on the Competing Values Framework" Addison-Wesley Publishing Company.

## Chapter 11

1. Seligman, Martin E.P., PhD. *Learned Optimism: How to Change your Mind and your Life*. 1998. New York. Pocket Books, a division of Simon & Schuster Inc.

## Chapter 13

1. Oliver, Gail. *Execume: It's More Than a Resume. It's a Reflection of You.* Atlanta: Empower You Publishers. 1999.
2. Repa, Barbara Kate, Attorney at Law, *Avoid Employee Lawsuits: Commonsense Tips for Responsible Management* http://www.nolo.com

## Chapter 14

1. Spencer, Lyle M., Jr., and Spencer, Signe M. *Competence at Work: Models for Superior Performance.* New York: John Wiley & Sons, Inc. 1993.
2. McClelland, David C. *Human Motivation.* Cambridge University Press 1988.

## Chapter 15

1. A general reference for published tests is Impala, James C., and Plake, Barbara S. (1998) *The thirteenth mental measurements yearbook.* Buros Institute. ISBN 091067454X.

## Chapter 16

1. Clark, Kim, Perry, Joellen, Melton, Melissa. "Why it pays to quit". *U.S. News & World Report.* November 1, 1999.
2. Conline, Michelle. "Give Me That Old-Time Economy". *Business Week.* April 24, 2000.
3. Author not available. "Global Survey Find Common Trends in Ways Top Companies Reward High Performers". *Business Wire.* May 22, 2000.
4. Stiffler, Mark A. "Incentive Compensation: The Pace of Change Continues to Accelerate". *Solutions.* May 2000.
5. O'Daniell, Ellen E. "Looking for Technology Talent? Fasten your seatbelt. It's about a lot more than money!" *Solutions.* May 2000.
6. Cook, John. "InfoSpace offers new kind of stake to keep employees". *Seattle Post-Intelligencer.* February 18, 2000.
7. Koss-Feder, Laura. "Time Select-Business: Easing Those Transfer Blues— Nowadays, your company's relocation policy can mean the difference between keeping or losing a good employee". *Time.* May 17, 1999.
8. Verespej, Michael A. "Balancing Act: In an effort to hire and retain employees companies are offering programs that help balance work and personal lives". *Industry Week.* May 15, 2000.

## Chapter 19

1. Brantley, Mary Ellen, Crowley, Robert, and Cook, Niki. *A Case Study in Executive Development.* 1997. International Society for Performance Improvement.

2. Brantley, Mary Ellen, Moore, John T., and Loscavio, Marie. *Leadership Competency Model*. Atlanta: BrantleyHouse 1998.

## Appendix

1. Wallace, Karen and Svenson, Ray, *Program Manager Performance Model* for Digital Equipment Corporation. 1990.
2. Brantley, Mary Ellen and Kirschbaum, Lila, PhD., *Project Manager Performance Model* 1991, Digital Equipment Corporation.
3. Brantley, Mary Ellen and Kirschbaum, Lila, PhD, *Performance Model for Consulting Services Principals*. 1992. Digital Equipment Corporation.
4. Brantley, Mary Ellen. "*Outsourcing Program Manager Performance Model.*" 1993. Digital Equipment Coporation.
5. Brantley, Mary Ellen and Kirschbaum, Lila, PhD. *A Performance model for Solutions Architects*. 1992. Digital Equipment Corporation.

# INDEX